THE 5 love LANGUAGES®

FOR MEN

Tools for Making a Good Relationship Great

Gary Chapman

with Randy Southern

NORTHFIELD PUBLISHING

CHICAGO

Portions of this book are from or adapted from the *5 Love Languages: Men's Edition*, © by Gary Chapman 2010.

Cover design: Faceout Studio
Cover photo: Boone Rodriguez (boonerodriguez.com)
Illustrations: © 2015 by Nathan Little (nathanlittleart.com). All rights reserved.
Author photo: P. S. Photography
Interior design: Smartt Guys design
Produced in association with Hudson Associates

Library of Congress Cataloging-in-Publication Data
Chapman, Gary D.
The five love languages for men: tools for making a good relationship great / Gary Chapman.
    p. cm.
Includes bibliographical references.
ISBN 978-0-8024-1272-0
1. Marriage. 2. Communication in marriage. 3. Love. 4. Husbands—Psychology. I. Title.
HQ734.C4554 2010
646.7'8—dc22

2009043037

We hope you enjoy this book from Northfield Publishing.
Our goal is to provide high-quality, thought-provoking books and products that connect truth to your real needs and challenges. For more information on other books and products that will help you with all your important relationships, go to 5lovelanguages.com or write to:

Northfield Publishing
820 N. LaSalle Blvd.
Chicago, IL 60610

1 3 5 7 9 10 8 6 4 2

Printed in the United States of America

Dedicated to the hundreds of men who have shared with me their struggles in trying to build a successful marriage

For a free online study guide, please visit
5lovelanguages.com

Contents

What's new in 5 Love Languages for Men?

On a light note, we've added some fun new stories that will give you insight into your own marriage, as well as artwork by the talented Nathan Little to illustrate the real-life challenges Dr. Chapman explores. But this revised and updated version of *5 Love Languages: Men's Edition* also tackles two new issues that must be addressed if the languages of love are to flow freely: dealing with anger and crafting apologies.

Learning to speak a new love language isn't easy. Trial and error is often the best strategy available to us, which can be frustrating. Add to that the vulnerability that comes from stepping outside our comfort zone, and you have the makings of a combustible situation. If our efforts to speak a love language fall short or fail to impress our spouse, we may be tempted to get angry.

And there's nothing wrong with that.

Anger isn't a sin. It's a natural response. What we do with that anger, though, makes all the difference in the world. If we learn to work through our anger in a healthy way, we'll find that the impact on our relationship is seismic.

In that same vein, mastering the art of the apology will go a long way toward ensuring the health of your marriage (and other relationships) for years to come.

Done well, an apology can bring closure to tensions, conflicts, and hurt feelings that have been sore spots for months, even years. It can change the way your spouse thinks of you—the way she looks at you. It can break down barriers faster than any other words or actions can.

With these two new tools to add to your love language workbench, you'll be better equipped than ever to make a difference in your spouse's life.

—RANDY SOUTHERN

THE 5 love LANGUAGES®

1

How Many Languages Do You Speak?

D id you hear about the guy who surprised his self-confessed "nerd" wife on their tenth anniversary with a geek-themed wedding reception? He spent *eighteen months* planning the party, which featured his wife's favorite pop-culture obsessions. The groomsmen wore superhero logos under their tuxes. Each tier of the wedding cake was dedicated to one of the couple's favorite movies or TV shows—*Superman, Star Wars, Firefly*, and *Dr. Who*—and decorated accordingly. The ring bearer, the couple's four-year-old son, wore a Superman cape. Somehow the guy managed to keep the whole thing a secret from his wife, even though all their friends and family were involved.

Then there was the guy who, for his one-year anniversary with his girlfriend, printed the story of how they fell in love on a bunch of flyers and posted them all over New York City. He asked people to take pictures of the flyers and post them on Instagram or Twitter, along with a certain hashtag. The whole thing went viral in a matter of hours. The couple received over a thousand photos, including some tweeted by celebrities such as Matt Lauer.

Or maybe you heard about the guy who created a book for his wife for their sixth anniversary. He spent an entire year writing 365 things he loved about his wife and then compiling the pages into one volume, along with photos of the two of them taken over the years.

Stories like these usually draw one of two reactions from fellow husbands. Either we tip our hats to these guys and give them kudos for their creativity (not to mention their fifteen minutes of fame), or we curse their names for blowing the curve and making the rest of us look lame by comparison.

Here's the kicker: **Unless those guys made their plans with their wives' primary love languages in mind, they could have achieved the same results with, say, generic greeting cards and Chinese takeout.**

IT'S NOT WHAT YOU SAY; IT'S THE LANGUAGE YOU USE

That's not a plug for Cantonese cuisine (though a good *dim sum* is never a bad thing)—or a knock against guys who try hard to impress their wives. Instead, it's an exclamation point on the importance of understanding love languages.

Everyone has a primary love language—a way of expressing devotion and affection that touches us deep inside, occasionally puts a goofy grin on our face, and leaves no doubt that we are truly and spectacularly loved.

As you probably deduced from the title of this book, there are five basic love languages:

1. Words of Affirmation (chapter 2)
2. Quality Time (chapter 3)
3. Gift Giving (chapter 4)
4. Acts of Service (chapter 5)
5. Physical Touch (chapter 6)

One of them is an expressway to your wife's heart. That's not to say she won't respond politely to one or more of the other languages, especially if she sees you making a real effort. Ultimately, though, those other four love languages are as foreign to her as Cantonese is to most native English speakers.

On the other hand, when you express your love for your wife using her *primary* love language, it's like hitting the sweet spot on a baseball bat or golf club. It just *feels right*—and the results are impressive.

THE NO-LOGIC ZONE

Logic suggests that men naturally gravitate toward women who share their primary love language—that quality timers pair up with quality timers and physical touchers have eyes only for other physical touchers; that with their shared love language, they communicate their affection easily and freely, forever and ever, amen.

Since when does logic have anything to do with love?

The truth is that people rarely marry partners who share their primary love language. Instead, guys who are built up by words of affirmation fall in love with girls who are built up through acts of service (or quality time or gift giving). Women who experience love primarily through gift giving are drawn to men who experience love through quality time (or physical touch or acts of service).

And a language barrier is created.

In the first stages of the relationship, when the couple is drunk with infatuation, they may not notice the language barrier. They may be so eager to please each other that they do things that are out of character—that is, they speak a love language they don't understand. They stay up all night talking about hopes and dreams. They take long walks, holding hands and walking with their arms around each other. They exchange small but meaningful presents.

Any concerns they may have about their differences get swept away in the tsunami of romance and excitement. The result? Two married people who speak and respond to different primary love languages.

> Even those rare couples who share a primary love language find that there are countless different "dialects" within each language. No two people share the same language *and* the same dialect. No two people express and receive love in exactly the same way.

If that seems like a blueprint for failure, consider this: In the club-houses of some of the most successful franchises in the NHL, MLB, and English Premier League, you can hear at least three (and probably more) different languages being spoken. The players on those teams *find* ways to communicate. People who are committed to excellence and success will not let a language barrier stand in their way.

WHEN THE HONEYMOON'S OVER

However, the obstacles are there. As the newness of the relationship wears off and the passion levels subside from their honeymoon crests, the two-language couple settles down into a routine. They go back to what they know best.

The acts of service–speaking husband gets busy showing his love for his wife in his "native tongue." He keeps her car serviced and clean. He tightens the washers on the leaky faucet. He repaints the bedroom and puts up new trim to match the room she saw and loved on HGTV.

Though his quality time–speaking wife appreciates the many things he does for her, she also pines for the long conversations they used to have when they were dating—the concentrated time and attention that feeds her soul. She longs for her husband to speak to her in her primary love language. As a result, her "love tank"—her reservoir of feeling genuinely adored, appreciated, and *known*— starts to empty.

How the scenario plays out from there depends on the couple. Some will chalk it up to the natural course of love and romance and settle for whatever is left. Some will blame the busyness and pressures of everyday life. Some will allow their frustrations and unmet needs to fester and spark conflicts and accusations. Some will suffer in silence, with each partner thinking something is wrong with him or her. Some will eventually convince themselves that they made a mistake in getting married in the first place.

There's no telling exactly what will happen when a person's love tank is empty.

WHERE THERE IS CHALLENGE, THERE IS OPPORTUNITY

Someone once said insanity is doing the same thing over and over again and expecting different results. If right, that means the approach many spouses take toward overcoming their language barrier is downright crazy. They double down on their own love language, trying over and over again to break through to their spouse in the only way they know. In other words, they work harder instead of smarter. They put the onus on their spouse to translate their actions into a language the spouse can understand.

Good intentions won't get the job done.

It doesn't matter that your heart is in the right place, or that you're trying as hard as you possibly can, or that other women would feel lucky to have a husband like you. You will not be able to fill your wife's love tank without using her primary love language.

The way to build a

thriving

exciting

unpredictable

awe-inspiring

life-changing

relationship with your wife is to master her primary love language, to embrace the challenge of becoming bilingual. The good news is that the process isn't nearly as challenging as learning an actual language. You don't have to worry about conjugating verbs or using the proper tense.

The challenge of becoming fluent in another love language might be better compared to perfecting a golf swing. If you've ever taken lessons from a pro, you know the first step is to "unlearn" all the

EQUIPPED FOR SUCCESS

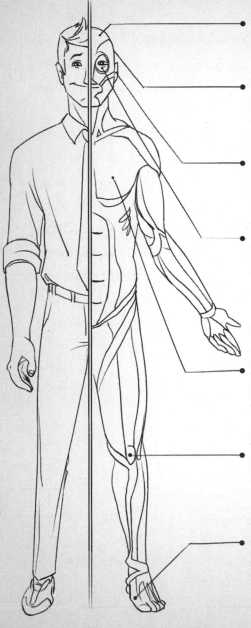

SHORT MEMORY
Not everything you try is going to work. In fact, your learning curve may be pretty steep. Keep in mind that whatever failure happened yesterday stays there. Today is a new day.

CREATIVITY
No idea is too off-the-wall or unconventional if it makes your wife feel truly loved. Thinking outside the box is highly encouraged.

LISTENING TO GOOD ADVICE
Don't miss opportunities to pick the brains of people whose relationships you admire. Press your role models for their secrets. See if there are any that will work for you and your wife.

VISION
The ability to spot new opportunities to show love to your wife—and to recognize whether old strategies are working—is key to becoming bilingual.

ENDURANCE
Mastering a new love language is a marathon, not a sprint. You'll get tired, discouraged, and frustrated along the way. Press on. And when you think you've got the language mastered, keep going. Keep learning. Keep trying new things. Keep finding new ways to make your wife feel loved.

PRAYER
You may not be a religious man, but when it comes to your relationship with your wife, you need all the help you can get. Don't be afraid to ask God for wisdom in how to effectively meet your wife's need for love.

FIRM STANCE
Nothing is more important than your relationship with your wife. Protecting and perfecting that relationship is Job One. Hold tight to that mindset and you'll set yourself up nicely for eventual success.

bad habits you've developed over the years. In many cases, that involves starting from scratch. The process is awkward at first. Things just don't feel right. They feel unnatural. Little by little, though, that starts to change. With enough repetition, you start to see positive results.

The same goes for learning a new love language. If you're an acts of service guy, you're probably not going to feel comfortable giving quality time to your wife. Not at first, at least. Your initial efforts likely will feel unnatural and forced.

But with the right attitude—and with the tips and strategies outlined in the pages that follow—you *will* master a second love language. You *will* fill your wife's love tank and keep it topped off. You *will* make her feel uniquely and spectacularly loved. You *will* experience what it's like to be on the top of your game, not just as a loving husband to your wife but also as a role model—to your children; to other young people who don't see that kind of behavior modeled in their own families; to other husbands who are looking for answers.

To become bilingual in the languages of love is to make a difference in other people's lives.

2

How to Become Fluent in Words of Affirmation

(LOVE LANGUAGE #1)

King Solomon, author of the ancient Hebrew Wisdom Literature, wrote, "The tongue has the power of life and death."

We can tell ourselves that Solomon was laying it on a little thick when he coined that phrase. But if you've ever received an exceptionally good review from a boss, you know how the tongue can add a little life to your step. Likewise, if you've ever been royally chewed out by a coach on the sidelines, you know what it is to die a thousand deaths in front of a home crowd.

Words can pack a punch.

If the movies have taught us anything, it's that **the right words, spoken at the right time by the right person, can inspire people to do the unlikely, the improbable, and in some cases, the near impossible.**

Think *Rocky II,* when Adrian, from her hospital bed, says, "There's one thing I want you to do for me: win. Win."

Think *Rudy,* when Fortune's verbal kick in the pants ("You're five-feet-nothin', a hundred and nothin'. And you got hardly a speck of athletic ability. And you hung in with the best college football team in the land for two years! . . . In this lifetime, you don't have to prove nothin' to nobody—except yourself!") stops Rudy from quitting the team.

Think *Hoosiers,* when Coach Dale's short motivational speech ("Forget about the crowds, the size of the school, their fancy uniforms, and remember what got you here . . . If you put your effort and concentration into playing to your potential, to be the best that you can be, I don't care what the scoreboard says at the end of the game. In my book, we're gonna be winners!") sets the stage for the greatest upset in the history of Indiana basketball.

It's this potential for good—the power of language to inspire, encourage, and build up—that makes words of affirmation such a vital tool on your marital workbench.

PUTTING IN A GOOD WORD

Mark Twain once said, "I can live for two months on a good compliment." Spoken like a true words of affirmation guy. His admission gets to the heart of this love language. For someone whose primary manner of receiving love is words of affirmation, compliments and encouragement aren't just nice gestures or polite conversational techniques.

They're nourishment.

That person doesn't just hear this:

"Well done!"

"You look incredible in that dress!"

"Attagirl!"

She also hears this:

"You have value."

"I love you."

"You make a difference."

The *real* power of words lies in their ability to fill people's love tanks. If your wife's primary love language is words of affirmation, that power is at your fingertips—or, more specifically, at the tip of your tongue.

How you feel about wielding that power will depend on your own primary love language. If you're the "strong, silent type," a guy who generally prefers to let his actions do the talking for him, learning to communicate through words of affirmation may prove to be a challenge. Then again, if you were the kind of guy who backs down from a challenge—especially where it concerns the love of your life—you probably wouldn't be reading this book.

You can become fluent in words of affirmation. Here are some tips to get you started.

FLATTERY WILL GET YOU NOWHERE

First things first: flattery is *not* a dialect of the words of affirmation love language. To the untrained ear, the two may *sound* similar, but there are several distinct—and important—differences between them. The quicker you recognize those differences, the fewer rookie mistakes you're likely to make as you strive for words of affirmation fluency.

Flattery is the language of manipulation. Flattery has an agenda. Its ultimate aim is to get something from the person being flattered—or to cast the flatterer in a positive light.

Flattery is the tool of lounge lizards ("Hey, baby, you look good. You wanna dance?") and apple-polishers (You're looking especially fit today, sir. Have you been working out?"). The more flattery your wife has been exposed to, the better she will be at recognizing—and dismissing—it. Flattery lacks the key ingredient of meaningful affirmation: sincerity. **If your words are going to make a difference in your wife's life, you have to *believe* what you say.**

Words of affirmation ≠ flattery.

Unlike shallow flattery, words of affirmation run deep. They spring from an intimate knowledge of the person being affirmed—in this case, your wife. Unlike flattery, words of affirmation don't arouse suspicion or put people on guard. Words of affirmation won't be met with a defensive posture or dismissed with an eye roll.

ALL JOKING ASIDE

Guys who are especially uncomfortable with verbal affirmation may be tempted to fall back on humor to ease the tension.

Resist that temptation.

What eases your discomfort may also cause some unintended pain for the person you're trying to affirm. The problem is, many people who are especially inspired or moved by words of affirmation are also especially susceptible to being hurt by less-than-loving words used in sarcasm, insults, and faint praise. Here are some examples:

- "It wasn't the *worst* meal I've ever had."
- "At least you get points for trying."
- "Not bad—for a thirty-five-year-old."

Such thoughtless, backhanded compliments can do more damage than you might imagine—and cause more pain than your wife might acknowledge.

"I was just kidding" is a pretty weak defense for throwing verbal dust in the face of someone who's thirsty for words of affirmation.

SENSES WORKING OVERTIME

Communicating love through words of affirmation involves more than your mouth; it also involves your eyes, your ears, your memory, your imagination, and more. In order to become fluent in this love language, you have to develop an extensive knowledge of—and appreciation for—the many things your wife does. In order to develop that appreciation, you have to watch her. In stealth mode, pay attention to the things she does, the things she says, the way she interacts with other people, the thankless jobs she tackles, and the ways she makes life better for you and others.

Keep a list of your observations on your phone or tablet. Make a point of adding to the list—big or small things—every day.

Your list might include things like the following:

- Knows when something's wrong with the kids
- Can make an old cutoff sweatshirt and shorts look good
- Always greets visitors at church
- Saves us money every week with her shopping skills
- Makes a better lasagna than any restaurant
- Never misses a bill payment; keeps our credit rating high
- Has great taste in music

After you deliver a compliment or words of affirmation based on an item on your list, delete it. This will ensure that you maintain a constant, fresh supply of affirmations to use.

WORKING THE GRAPEVINE

What's better—having someone high-five you after a pickup game and say, "Good job," or walking into a gym and having someone point to you and say, "I hear that guy's got some serious game"?

In both scenarios, you're getting complimented. But the second scenario carries with it some fame and notoriety, which only sweetens the pot.

Discovering that people are talking about you—in a good way— makes any day better. With that in mind, look for ways to send words of affirmation "through the grapevine" to your wife. Talk her up around other people when she's not around. Publicize her accomplishments and skills. Help others recognize how incredible she is. (All things in moderation, of course. You'll want to be careful not to become "that guy"—the one people try to avoid because they're tired of hearing about his practically perfect wife.)

You won't be able to control which words of affirmation actually make it back to your wife. But you can direct your comments to the people most likely to spill the beans: your kids, other family members, your mutual friends, her coworkers, and anyone else who spends a lot of time with her.

Don't hide your admiration, appreciation, and awe for your wife from the people you know.

Along those same lines, public affirmations can go a long way toward filling your wife's love tank. Look for opportunities to talk her up when the two of you are with friends or acquaintances.

During a dinner out with coworkers, you might say something like, "I thought the tiramisu was pretty good, but if I could have any dessert in the world, it would be my wife's peach cobbler."

A Lesson They'll Never Forget

Want to set a powerful and lasting example for your kids? Tell them how great their mother is. Be specific, genuine, and generous with your praise. Leave no doubt as to how blessed you are to be her husband.

Done right, your words may inspire your sons to heap similar affirmation on their wives when they get married—and inspire your daughters to look for husbands who will do the same for them.

WHERE OFTEN IS HEARD AN ENCOURAGING WORD

Some of the best opportunities in life involve risk—the very real possibility of rejection, embarrassment, or failure. It takes a lot of courage to roll the dice and face the possible consequences. Those who choose to pursue those opportunities usually face no shortage of discouragers—people inclined to rain on their parade and argue that something can't be done or shouldn't be tried. These doom-and-gloom promoters can be pretty persuasive, especially if there's no one to counter their influence.

Cue the encouraging spouse.

Your wife likely has untapped potential in one or more areas of life. That potential may be awaiting your encouraging words. Perhaps she needs to enroll in a course to develop that potential. Maybe she needs to meet some people who have succeeded in that area and can give her insight on the next step she needs to take. Your words may give your wife the courage necessary to take that first step.

Let's be clear: I'm *not* talking about pressuring your wife to do something that *you* want. I'm talking about encouraging her to develop an interest that she already has. A certain well-meaning husband may be tempted to pressure his wife to look for a more lucrative job. He may think he's encouraging her, but unless that's what she wants too, his words will sound more like condemnation to her. If she has the desire and motivation to seek a better position, her husband's words will bolster her resolve. If not, his words will come across as judgmental and guilt inducing. They will express not love but rejection.

If, however, she says, "You know, I've been thinking about starting a catering business on the side," then he has the opportunity to give words of encouragement ("If you decide to do that, I can tell you one thing: you'll be a success. That's one of the things I love about you. When you set your mind to something, you do it. If that's what you want to do, I'll certainly do everything I can to help you"). Such words may give her the courage to start drawing up a list of potential clients.

Encouragement requires empathy—seeing the world from your wife's perspective. We must first learn what is important to our wives. Only then can we give encouragement. With verbal encouragement, we're trying to communicate, "I know. I care. I'm with you. How can I help?" We're trying to show that we believe in her and in her abilities. We're giving credit and praise.

Most of us have more potential than we'll ever develop. What holds us back is often a lack of courage. A loving spouse can supply that all-important catalyst.

THE WAY YOU SAY THE THINGS YOU SAY

Becoming fluent in words of affirmation requires more than just mastering compliments and encouragement. It also involves communicating with a tone and an attitude that are unmistakably loving. What does this type of tone and attitude sound like? Well, for starters . . .

"Love is kind."

That's not some sappy greeting card sentiment. Kindness is essential to healthy relationships. **Speaking kindly to your wife means making sure your words and tone align.** Seems like a simple thing, but it can be a challenge for a lot of guys. From an early age, we're conditioned to wield words like weapons. Sarcasm comes easily to us. We use taunts to good-naturedly (and sometimes not-so-good-naturedly) give others the business. If we're standing in a tee box with a friend/competitor who's just sliced his drive two fairways over, it takes real restraint not to say something like, "Nicely played, Tiger."

As we mentioned earlier, what seems like good-natured ribbing to some people can have a much different effect on someone whose primary way of receiving love is through genuine, heartfelt communication. To her, such tactics will seem anything but kind.

Maintaining the right tone and attitude is especially important when you're feeling annoyed or angry. Snarling, "I would be delighted to wash dishes tonight"—in a tone dripping with sarcasm—will *not* be received as an expression of love, no matter how clean you get the pans. On the other hand, saying something as pointed as, "I felt disappointed and hurt that you didn't offer to help me this evening"—in an honest, kind manner—can be an expression of love.

With your tone and attitude, you're telling your wife that you want to be known by her. You're taking steps to build intimacy by sharing your feelings. You're asking for an opportunity to discuss a hurt in order to find healing. Those same words, delivered in a loud, harsh voice, will not be received as an expression of love but as an expression of condemnation and judgment.

The hotter a situation gets, the more of an impact kindness will have. When your wife is angry, upset, and lashing out with provocative words, try responding with a soft, calm voice. Take in everything she has to say about her emotions and feelings. Let her tell you of her hurt, anger, and perception of events. Work hard to put yourself in her shoes and see the situation through her eyes. Express softly and kindly your understanding of why she feels that way. If you've wronged her, be willing to confess the wrong and ask for forgiveness. If your motivation is different from what she's reading, explain your real motivation kindly. **Your goal must be to achieve understanding and reconciliation, not to prove your own correctness or superiority.**

Another principle comes into play as we work to become fluent in the kindness dialect of words of affirmation. Put simply, love doesn't keep a score of wrongs; it doesn't bring up past failures.

In marriage we don't always do the right (or best) thing. We sometimes say hurtful things to our spouses. We can't erase the past. We can only confess it and agree that it was wrong. We can ask for forgiveness and try to act differently in the future. Having apologized and asked for forgiveness, I can ask if there is anything else I might do to mitigate the hurt I may have caused my wife. When I've been wronged by my wife and she has painfully apologized and requested forgiveness, I have the option of justice or forgiveness. If I choose justice and seek to pay her back or make her pay for her wrongdoing, I'm making

Spoiler Alert: None of us is perfect.

myself the judge and treating her as the felon. Intimacy becomes impossible. If, however, I choose to forgive, intimacy can be restored. Forgiveness is the way of love.

I am amazed by how many individuals mess up every new day with yesterday. They insist on bringing into today the failures of yesterday. In so doing, they pollute a potentially wonderful day. "I can't believe you did it. I don't think I'll ever forget it. You can't possibly know how much you hurt me. I don't know how you can sit there so smugly after you treated me that way. You ought to be crawling on your knees, begging me for forgiveness. I don't know if I can ever forgive you." Those are not the words of love but of bitterness, resentment, and revenge. The best thing we can do with the failures of the past is to let them be history. Yes, it happened. Certainly it hurt. And it may still hurt, but she's acknowledged her failure and asked for your forgiveness. We can't erase the past, but we can accept it as history. We can choose to live today free from the failures of yesterday.

Forgiveness isn't a feeling; it's a commitment. It's a choice to show mercy, not to hold the offense up against the offender. Forgiveness is an expression of love. "I love you. I care about you, and I choose to forgive you. Even though my feelings of hurt may linger, I won't allow what's happened to come between us. I hope we can learn from this experience. You're not a failure because you've failed. You're my wife, and together we'll go on from here." Those are words of affirmation expressed in the dialect of kindness.

A LITTLE HUMILITY GOES A LONG WAY

The final dialect of words of affirmation that we'll be looking at in this chapter is humility. Love makes requests, not demands. When I demand things from my wife, I become a parent and she the child. In marriage, however, we are equal, adult partners. We're not perfect, to be sure, but we are adults and we are partners. If we're to develop an intimate relationship, we need to know each other's desires. If we wish to love each other, we need to know what the other person wants.

The way we express those desires, however, is all-important. If they come across as demands, we have erased the possibility of intimacy and will drive our spouse away. If, however, we make our needs and desires known in the form of a request, we're giving guidance, not ultimatums. The husband who says, "Could you make that good pasta one of these nights?" is giving his wife guidance on how to love him and thus build intimacy. On the other hand, the husband who says, "Can't we ever have a decent meal around here?" is showing adolescent behavior by making a demand. His wife is likely to fire back, "If you don't like what I make, you cook!"

When you make a request of your wife, you're affirming her worth and abilities. You're indicating that she has or can do something that's meaningful and worthwhile to you. When you make demands, you become not a lover but a tyrant. Your wife won't feel affirmed; she'll feel belittled.

A request introduces the element of choice. Your wife may choose to respond to your request or to deny it, because love is always a choice. That's what makes it meaningful. To know that my wife loves me enough to respond to one of my requests communicates emotionally that she cares about me, respects me, admires me, and wants to do something to please me. We cannot get emotional love by way of demand. My wife may in fact comply with my demands, but it's not an expression of love. It's an act of fear or guilt or some other emotion, but not love. A request creates the possibility for an expression of love; a demand suffocates that possibility.

The more you work these essentials of words of affirmation into your daily interaction with your wife, the more fluent you'll become—and the more positive changes you'll see in your relationship.

WORDS OF AFFIRMATION PHRASE BOOK

With dedication and practice, you can become fluent in words of affirmation. Along the way, you may need some assistance—ideas to use when you're unable to come up with one of your own. Here are some suggestions for just such an occasion.

■ Don't just say, "You look good." Say, "That's a nice color on you" or "I like your hair that way." **Compliment a different physical feature** each day this week.

■ **Make a habit of mentioning something specific you've observed** that has to do with who she is. Examples: "I meant to tell you, I really loved how you talked with that elderly woman after church." Or, "I enjoy taking walks with you. You always point out interesting things."

■ Initiate conversations to encourage her to share her inner dreams and desires. **Begin a campaign of verbal affirmation to inspire courage** for her to take steps to make those dreams come true.

■ Add your own observations that might **help your wife identify her skills and strengths**. For example, "I've never heard you express an interest in teaching, but from the way you handle the kids, I think you would make a terrific teacher."

■ If you're artistic, **create a poster or print with her name in the center** surrounded by descriptive words, phrases, and special names you have for her. If you're not so artistic, use old magazines and newspapers to cut and paste ransom-note-like messages of affirmation for her.

■ **Create a playlist for your wife**. You can be the DJ, explaining why you included each song.

- **Send her an encouraging email**, particularly if you know she might be having a hard day. Put in a link to an amusing website.

- Think of every recent argument or problem the two of you have had and **try to clear the air**.

- Learn how to **say "I love you" or other expressions of affirmation in a different language**.

- **Thank her for something she does routinely** and probably doesn't even expect to be complimented for.

3

How to Become Fluent in Quality Time

(Love Language #2)

———————

Time may or may not be the most precious asset we possess. (If you're scrambling to pay your mortgage or trying to figure out how to afford college, you can probably build a pretty solid case in favor of money.) But time *is* unique among our commodities.

Every day, every person who draws breath on this earth receives the same amount of time: 24 hours, 1,440 minutes, or 86,400 seconds, depending on which denomination you prefer.

At the end of every day, every person's allotment is depleted. Time cannot be rolled over or stockpiled. When it's gone, it's gone.

Time cannot be stolen or transferred into another account. Its market cannot be cornered. The rich cannot get richer, where time is concerned. Its system cannot be gamed, hacked, or tampered with.

Time cannot be exchanged or refunded.

Time is extremely limited—yet insanely in demand. Think of the things that are competing for your time:

Your job.

Your overtime demands and opportunities.

Your commute.

Your workout.

Your responsibilities as a friend, neighbor, church member, and concerned citizen.

Your kids' practices, games, recitals, and programs.

Your hobbies and pastimes.

Your body's requirements for sleep and relaxation.

So many options, so little time to explore them all.

No one understands that truth better than a person whose primary love language is quality time.

If you're married to a native quality time speaker, you should feel at least a little flattered. Your wife isn't looking for words of affirmation or gifts or acts of service. She just wants you. She will experience love and affection—she will feel genuinely cared for— simply by sharing some of your precious time. A half hour here, an hour there, or a weekend on occasion is enough to keep her love tank filled.

Provided it's the right kind of time.

THE RIGHT KIND OF TIME

Quality is the key. To call something "quality" is to set a high bar. A mechanic who does quality work doesn't cut corners on a brake job. He isn't distracted while he rebuilds a carburetor. He won't throw up his hands and walk away when he can't immediately pinpoint a rattle in the exhaust system.

Someone who does quality work goes the extra mile, stays focused on the task at hand, and won't quit when things don't go right.

And so it is with spending quality time with your wife. When you give it, make sure it's the best you've got. Here's how.

DEEP FOCUS

The key to becoming fluent in the quality time love language is establishing the right mindset. The key to establishing the right mindset is focused attention.

Some husbands and wives think they're spending time together when, in reality, they're only living in close proximity. They're in the same house at the same time, but they're not together. A husband who is texting while his wife tries to talk to him isn't giving her quality time, because she doesn't have his full attention.

That's not to say quality time means spending your together moments gazing into each other's eyes. It means doing something

together and giving your full attention to each other. The activity in which you're both engaged is incidental. The important thing emotionally is that you're spending focused time in each other's company. The activity is a vehicle that creates the sense of togetherness.

A husband and wife playing tennis together, if it's genuine quality time, will focus not on the game but on the fact that they're spending time together. What happens on the emotional level is what matters. Spending time together in a common pursuit communicates that you care about each other, that you enjoy being with each other, that you like to do things together.

PUTTING THE QUALITY IN CONVERSATION

Like words of affirmation, the language of quality time has many dialects. One of the most common dialects is quality conversation—that is, a genuine dialogue in which you share experiences, thoughts, feelings, and desires in a friendly, uninterrupted context. To engage in quality conversation is to say

- "I will focus on drawing you out";
- "I will listen sympathetically to what you have to say";
- "I will ask questions—not in a badgering manner but with a real desire to understand you."

Most people who complain that their spouses don't talk don't mean literally that their spouses never say a word. They mean their spouses seldom take part in sympathetic dialogue. If your wife's primary love language is quality time, such dialogue is crucial to her emotional sense of being loved.

I met Patrick when he was forty-three and had been married for seventeen years. I remember him because his first words were so dramatic. He sat in the leather chair in my office; after briefly intro-ducing himself, he leaned forward and said with great emotion, "Dr. Chapman, I have been a fool, a real fool."

"What led you to that conclusion?" I asked.

"I've been married for seventeen years," he said, "and my wife has left me. Now I realize what a fool I've been."

I rephrased my original question. "In what way have you been a fool?"

"My wife would come home from work and tell me about the problems in her office," he explained. "I would listen to her and then tell her what I thought she should do. I always gave her advice. I told her she had to confront the problem. 'Problems don't go away. You have to talk with the people involved or your supervisor. You have to deal with problems.' The next day she would come home from work and tell me about the same problems. I would ask her if she did what I'd suggested the day before. She would shake her head and say no. So I'd repeat my advice. I told her that was the way to deal with the situ-ation. She would come home the next day and tell me about the same problems. Again I would ask her if she had done what I'd suggested. She would shake her head and say no.

"After three or four nights of that, I got angry. I told her not to expect any sympathy from me if she wasn't willing to take the advice I was giving her. She didn't have to live under that kind of stress and pressure. She could solve the problem if she would simply do what I told her. It hurt me to see her living under such stress because I knew she didn't have to. The next time she brought up the problem, I said, 'I don't want to hear about it. I've told you what you need to do. If you're not going to listen to my advice, I don't want to hear it.'

"I withdrew and went about my business. Now I realize that she didn't want advice when she told me about her struggles at work. She wanted sympathy. She wanted me to listen, to give her attention, to let her know that I could understand the hurt, the stress, the pressure. She wanted to know that I loved her and that I was with her. She didn't want advice; she just wanted to know that I understood. But I never tried to understand. I was too busy giving advice. And now she's gone.

"Why can't you see these things when you're going through them?" he asked. "I was blind to what was going on. Only now do I understand how I failed her."

Patrick's wife had been pleading for quality conversation. Emotionally, she longed for him to focus attention on her by listening to her pain and frustration. Patrick wasn't focusing on listening but on speaking. He listened only long enough to hear the problem and formulate a solution. He didn't listen long enough or well enough to hear her cry for support and understanding.

Anyone care to cast the first stone here?

The truth is, many of us are like Patrick. We're trained to analyze problems and create solutions. We lose sight of the fact that marriage is a relationship, not a project to be completed or a problem to be solved. A relationship calls for sympathetic listening with a view to understanding the other person's thoughts, feelings, and desires. We may give advice— but only when it's requested and never in a condescending manner.

Most of us have little training in listening. We're far more proficient in thinking and speaking. That lack of training will be hard to hide if your wife's primary love language is quality time and her dialect is quality conversation. Fortunately, listening is a skill that can be acquired fairly quickly (though it takes years to master). Here are some practical tips to get you started.

1. **Maintain eye contact when your wife is talking.** That keeps your mind from wandering and communicates that she has your full attention.

2. **Don't listen to your wife and do something else at the same time.** Remember, quality time is giving someone your undivided attention. If you're doing something you can't turn from immediately, tell your wife the truth. A positive approach might be, "I know you're trying to talk to me, and I'm interested, but I want to give you my full attention. I can't do that right now, but if you'll give me ten minutes to finish this, I'll sit down and listen to you." Most wives will respect such a request.

3. **Listen for feelings.** Ask yourself, "What emotion is my wife experiencing?" When you think you have the answer, confirm

it. For example, "It sounds to me like you're feeling disappointed because I forgot _____." That gives her the chance to clarify her feelings. It also communicates that you're listening intently to what she's saying.

4. **Observe body language.** Clenched fists, trembling hands, tears, furrowed brows, and eye movement may give you clues as to what she's feeling. Sometimes body language speaks one message while words speak another. Ask for clarification to make sure you know what she's really thinking and feeling.

5. **Refuse to interrupt.** If you give your undivided attention while your wife is talking, you will refrain from defending yourself, hurling accusations, or dogmatically stating your position. Your goal will be to discover your wife's thoughts and feelings.

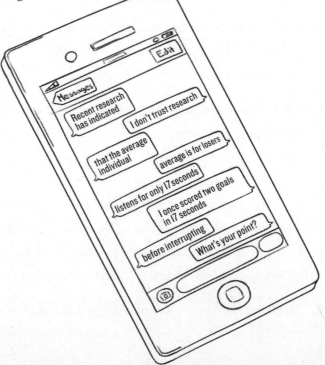

OPEN UP

Quality conversation requires not only sympathetic listening but also self-revelation. When a wife says, "I wish my husband would talk. I never know what he's thinking or feeling," she's pleading for intimacy. She wants to feel close to her husband, but how can she feel close to someone who's a silent mystery? In order for her to feel loved, he must learn to reveal himself. If her primary love language is quality time and her dialect is quality conversation, her emotional love tank will never be filled until he tells her his thoughts and feelings.

Think of it in terms of a tennis game. If one person is doing everything, the result is simply ace after ace. What could be more boring or less engaging—for either player? If, on the other hand, Player 2 starts *returning* the serve, it's game on. Back and forth. Each of you receiving what the other is offering—and then sending it back with your own spin on it. Before you know it, you find yourself in the middle of some long, satisfying volleys.

If only quality conversation were as easy as returning a tennis serve.

Self-revelation is a challenge for many guys. Some adults grew up in homes where the expression of thoughts and feelings were discouraged. To request a toy was to receive a lecture on the sad state of family finances. The child went away feeling guilty for having the desire, and he quickly learned not to express his desires. When he expressed anger, the parents responded with harsh and condemning words. Thus, the child learned that expressing angry feelings isn't appropriate. If the child was made to feel guilty for expressing disappointment at, say, not being able to go to the store with his father, he learned to hold his disappointment inside. By the time we reach adulthood, many of us have learned to deny our feelings. We're no longer in touch with our emotional selves.

A wife says to her husband, "How did you feel about what Steve did?" The husband responds, "I think he was wrong. He should have . . ." But he's not telling her his feelings. He's voicing his thoughts. Perhaps he has reason to feel angry, hurt, or disappointed, but he's lived so long in the world of thought that he doesn't acknowledge his feelings. If that describes you, then learning the language of quality conversation will be like learning a foreign language. The way to begin is to get in touch with your feelings—to become aware that you're an emotional creature, despite having denied that part of your life.

A great first step is to keep track of the emotions you feel away from home. Carry a small notepad with you. Three times each day, ask yourself, "What emotions have I felt in the last three hours?" Ask yourself specific questions: "What did I feel on the way to work when the driver behind me was riding my bumper? What did I feel when I stopped at the gas station and the automatic pump didn't shut off and covered the side of my car with gas? What did I feel when I got to the office and found out the project I was working on had to be completed in three days when I thought I had another two weeks?"

Write down your feelings in the notepad and a word or two to help you remember the event corresponding to the feeling. Your list may look like this:

Event	Feelings
Tailgater	Angry
Gas station	Very upset
Work project due in 3 days	Frustrated and anxious

Do that exercise three times a day and you'll start to develop an awareness of your emotional nature. Using your notepad, communicate your emotions (and the events that inspired them) briefly to your wife as many days as possible. In a few weeks, you'll become comfortable expressing your emotions with her. Eventually you'll feel comfortable discussing your emotions toward your wife, the children, and events that occur in your home. Remember, emotions themselves are neither good nor bad. They're simply our psychological responses to the events of life.

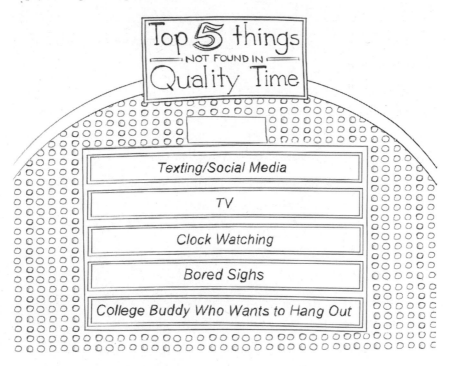

Top **5** things
— NOT FOUND IN —
Quality Time

- Texting/Social Media
- TV
- Clock Watching
- Bored Sighs
- College Buddy Who Wants to Hang Out

QUALITY ACTIVITIES

Another dialect of quality time is quality activities. At a recent marriage seminar, I asked couples to complete the following sentence: "I feel most loved by my husband/wife when _____." Here's the response of a twenty-nine-year-old husband who had been married for eight years.

> *I feel most loved by my wife when we do things together, things I like to do and things she likes to do. We talk more. It sorta feels like we are dating again.*

That's a typical response of individuals whose primary love language is quality time. The emphasis is on being together, doing things together, giving each other undivided attention.

Quality activities may include anything in which one or both of you have an interest. The emphasis is not on what you're doing but on *why* you're doing it. The purpose is to experience something together, to have your wife walk away from it, thinking, *He cares about me. He was willing to do something with me that I enjoy, and he did it with a positive attitude.* That is love, and for some people it is love's loudest voice.

Quality activities may include such things as putting in a garden, visiting Civil War battlefields, going to a concert, training for a 5K, or having another couple over for pizza and games. The possibilities are limited only by your interest and willingness to try new experiences. These are the essential aspects of a quality activity:

At least one of you wants to do it.

The other is willing to do it.

Both of you know *why* you're doing it—that is, to express love by being together.

One of the by-products of quality activities is that they provide a memory bank from which to draw in the years ahead. You'll get to be one of those couples who remembers an early morning stroll along the coast, the spring they planted the flower garden, the time they got poison ivy chasing the rabbit through the woods, the night they attended their first major-league ballgame together, the ski trip that got cut short by a broken leg suffered in the lodge, the amusement parks, the concerts, the cathedrals, and the awe of standing beneath the waterfall after a two-mile hike. Those are memories of love, especially for the person whose primary love language is quality time.

Quality time pays for itself in memories.

Where do you find time for such activities, especially if you both have careers outside the home? You *make* time, just as you make time for lunch and dinner. Why? Because it's just as essential to your marriage as meals are to your health. Is it difficult? Does it take careful planning? Yes. Does it mean you have to give up some individual activities? Perhaps. Does it mean you do some things you don't particularly enjoy? Certainly. Is it worth it? Without a doubt. What's in it for you? The pleasure of living with a wife who feels loved and knowing that you learned to speak her love language fluently.

QUALITY TIME PHRASE BOOK

Congratulations on learning to speak the love language of quality time! Certainly no one can be expected to master a new way of communicating overnight. For those times when you can't come up with the right idea, here are a few to consider.

- Respect the "early bird" or "night owl" tendencies of your wife. **Plan your quality times according to her schedule**. Set your alarm earlier or drink coffee to stay up later—whatever it takes for her to feel your time together is special.

- **Sacrifice something you love to create time to share with her**: give up a Saturday-morning golf game, drop out of the church basketball league for a season, skip a nonessential business commitment. Doing this will send a powerful message that she matters more than these things.

- **Make lists of "Our Top 10 Moments Together as a Couple."** When you finish, compare your lists to see how many of your favorite memories overlap.

- Many men need to "unlearn" inattentiveness. **If you find it hard to devote full attention to any single thing, practice by listening** to your kids when they're extra chatty, paying close attention to the Sunday sermon from beginning to end, or listening to music without allowing your mind to wander.

- Some couples are together a lot more than others. If that's the case for you, don't try to make all your time together "quality time." **Designate specific times and places for planned togetherness**.

- If your wife is the one who's usually pressed for time, perhaps you can **occasionally do one (or more) of her dreaded, time-consuming chores**. Pay the bills, run the errands, put the kids to bed—and free her up for some quality time.

- **Find an activity you like to do that complements something your wife enjoys** so that you can spend more time together. If she likes to go to the gym and you like to play computer games, you get little quality time together. But if you're willing to go to the gym with her or to take up something new you can do together—such as geo-caching or gourmet cooking—you'll add a new dimension to your relationship.

- If you're a couple who have moved beyond the newlywed stage, it's likely that much of your time—and conversation—is focused on life's mechanics: When does the dog go to the vet? Where's the window spray? How much should you pay for a new garbage disposal? Try monitoring your conversations in order to **make sure all your time and talk isn't swallowed up by your to-do list**.

- **Surprise her with two tickets to a movie** you know she would particularly enjoy. Afterward take her to dinner and ask her to share her review of the movie.

- If you're in the habit of praying as a couple, add a little additional time for togetherness. **While you're spending quality time with God, spend quality time with each other**.

- If your schedules permit, look for opportunities to take a "snow day" or "summer vacation day." **Forget what you had planned and do something—anything—spontaneous**.

- **Take turns selecting books to read**. Designate pages or chapters to read individually on your own time, and then discuss the content during your quality time together. Or read aloud to each other.

- Car trips tend to promote conversation between couples, so **take a long drive**. You might travel to a favorite restaurant two or three hours away, have lunch, and then drive back.

- If you run out of things to say, **learn to enjoy silence together**. Set a timer and agree not to say anything as you watch a sunset or walk through the woods.

- You have to do chores anyway, so why not make them a time for quality conversation? **Share tasks like cleaning house, and talk** as you dust, mop, and put things away.

RECEIVING GIFTS

4

How to Become Fluent in Gift Giving

(LOVE LANGUAGE #3)

Erik spent a year in Kelsey's "friend zone" before she agreed to go out with him. Since they were both big baseball fans, Erik took her to an Indianapolis Indians game for their first date. The Indians' minor league stadium allows fans to sit on grassy hills rather than outfield bleachers. Erik and Kelsey were enjoying a picnic dinner just beyond the left-field fence when the Indians' first baseman drove a hanging curveball their way. Erik jumped up and made an impressive bare-handed catch—his first home-run grab ever.

Two days later, Kelsey found a gift-wrapped package outside her dorm room. She opened it and found a baseball in a small plastic display case (the kind collectors use). Taped to the inside of the case was a ticket stub from the game. Inscribed on the ball was the date of the game and these words:

1st home-run catch
2nd best thing to happen to me that day

Within two years of their first date, Erik and Kelsey were married. Today, some fifteen years later, that baseball, still in its display case, sits on Kelsey's bedroom dresser, where she can see it every day. Recently one of her friends asked her which possession she would grab first if her house were on fire. Kelsey's reply?

"The baseball Erik gave me."

At a garage sale, that ball and its case might go for a buck, maybe a buck and a half. But Kelsey wouldn't part with it for a thousand times that amount.

Behold the power of a thoughtful gift.

THE CART AND THE HORSE

If Kelsey's primary love language had been words of affirmation, quality time, acts of service, or physical touch, Erik's gift might have been met with a blank stare or a halfhearted thank-you. But Erik rolled the dice on gift giving and walked away a big winner.

Kelsey was overwhelmed by the fact that he gave up his home-run ball, wrote a heartfelt note, commemorated the date of their first outing as a couple, and packaged the whole thing in such a way that it stayed visible *and* protected. All for her.

The fact that Erik could speak her love language so early in their relationship gave Kelsey hope that he might be The One. Turns out she was right.

Not everyone picks up the language as quickly as Erik did. Then again, not everyone is as motivated to become fluent as Erik was.

Of the five love languages, gift giving is the one most likely to raise an eyebrow or two. In some circles, drawing any connection between love and gifts is enough to inspire whispers of materialism, gold digging, or worse. That's why it's important to emphasize from the start which is the cart (gifts) and which is the horse (love).

Love is what drives a husband to learn his wife's primary love language. His aim is to demonstrate his love in a way that she understands and appreciates. To be clear: the love between them is already there. He's not trying to "earn" his wife's affection by buying her expensive gifts. He's expressing what's in his heart in the way she experiences love most intensely.

Likewise, a person whose primary love language is gift giving is not necessarily a materialistic person. **Her aim is not to amass a collection of valuables but rather to surround herself with reminders of her loved one's affection.** The cost and worth of the presents are incidental to her. When it comes to the gift giving love language, it truly is the thought that counts.

TANGIBLE EXPRESSIONS

The connection between love and gifts is more deeply rooted than most people realize. How old were you the first time you picked a flower or dandelion and gave it to your mom as a present—a way of saying, "I love you"? How many knickknacks did you create for your parents at camp, in Sunday school, or in art class?

The instincts are there. Harnessing and perfecting those natural inclinations is the key to becoming fluent in the love language of gift giving.

The notion that delighted your parents all those years ago (and perhaps still does) runs strong in people whose primary love language is gift giving. A gift is something they can hold in their hands as they say, "Look, he was thinking of me." Therein lies the appeal. **You have to *think* of someone before you give her a gift. The gift itself is a symbol of that thought.** It doesn't matter whether it costs money.

What's important is that you thought of her—that you took the time to consider what would make her happy and then followed through.

Storytellers

Want to add a little something extra to your gift? Give it a story. A stuffed bear holding a sign that says, "I [HEART] West Virginia" is one thing. A stuffed, sign-wielding bear purchased in a gift shop on the very block where your wife's great-grandmother's house once stood—which you know because you did some genealogical research before your trip—is quite another.

Of course, not every story needs to be so dramatic or involve such effort. A simple "I heard you say you wanted to try something new in the kitchen, so I bought you a Cajun cookbook" or "I made a playlist of some of the new songs you've been singing along to lately" will do nicely.

An effective story-gift combo is one that gives your wife some insight into the way your mind works when it's thinking about her.

Gifts are visual symbols of love. The importance of such symbols may be lost on nonnative speakers of the gift giving love language. The difference between the native and nonnative mindsets can be seen in people's attitudes toward the most common visual symbol of love in our culture: the wedding ring. Most wedding ceremonies include the giving and receiving of rings. The person performing the ceremony says something to the effect of, "These rings are outward and visible signs of an inward and spiritual bond that unites your two

hearts in love that has no end." That's not meaningless rhetoric. Those words give power to the visual symbol of the union—especially where native speakers of gift giving are concerned.

That's why some people never take their ring off after the wedding. If gift giving is your wife's primary love language but not yours, she probably wears her ring more often—and spends more time thinking about it—than you do. She likely places great value on her ring—and wears it with tremendous pride—because *you* gave it to her as an enduring symbol of your love. She's also probably been moved by other gifts you've given her through the years. She views them as expressions of your love.

WHAT THAT MEANS FOR YOU

To take that point one step further: *without* **gifts as visual symbols, your wife may question your love.**

For some of you, that last sentence triggered alarm bells in your head. Or the *cha-ching* of a cash register. Maybe you did a quick check to see if this chapter is being underwritten by Hallmark, ProFlowers, or Kay Jewelers.

So let's reiterate the point made earlier: generally speaking, a gift's impact has nothing to do with its cost or worth.

Great gifts come in all sizes, colors, and shapes. Some are expensive, and others are free. If your wife's primary love language is gift giving, **the cost of the gift will matter to her only if it's greatly out of line with what you can afford—or what you spend on yourself or others.**

If you live on a golf course in a gated community and treat yourself to a new car every year, you can't come home every week with gifts you picked up from a dollar store and expect them to convey genuine love and affection for your wife. If, on the other hand, your household finances are in dire shape, a well-chosen gift from a dollar store may speak a million dollars' worth of love.

> **If your wife is consistently critical and unappreciative of the gifts you give, you may want to reevaluate. Gift giving is almost certainly not her primary love language.**

Gifts may be purchased, found, or made. If you see an interesting bird feather while you're out running and bring it home to your wife . . . guess what? You've given her an expression of love. A five-dollar greeting card that catches your eye and conveys your feelings would make an ideal gift. If your budget doesn't allow for a five-dollar-card expenditure, a card designed and written by you on a piece of computer paper would make an equally ideal gift.

What could be simpler?

SAVERS AND SPENDERS

Still, not everyone is convinced that gift giving is a meaningful way to speak love. Some try to pass off their reluctance as financial "wisdom."

Each of us has particular thoughts about the purpose of money, as well as particular emotions associated with spending it. Some people have a spending orientation. They feel good about themselves when they're using money to buy things they need—or want. Others have a saving and investing orientation. They feel good about themselves when they hold on to their money and make it work for them by investing wisely.

If you're a spender by nature, you'll likely have little difficulty purchasing gifts for your wife. If you're a saver, though, you may experience some intellectual or emotional resistance to the idea. After all, if you don't purchase things for yourself, why should you purchase things for your wife?

That kind of thinking makes such good financial sense that it can be hard to see how emotionally skewed it is. The truth is, **if you're a saver, you *are* (in a sense) purchasing things for yourself. By holding on to your money, you're "purchasing" self-worth and security.** You're using your assets to care for your own emotional needs.

What you're *not* doing is meeting the emotional needs of your wife.

If your wife's primary love language is gift giving, you must recognize that buying gifts for her is the best long-range plan in your portfolio. You are investing in your relationship and filling your wife's emotional love tank. With a full love tank, she will likely reciprocate emotional love to you in a language *you'll* understand. That's what's known as a win-win.

When both persons' emotional needs are met, your marriage will take on a whole new dimension. To invest in loving your wife is to invest in the bluest of blue-chip stocks.

The Perfect Gift

We wouldn't waste a sidebar to suggest something as obvious as buying jewelry for your wife. However, we will suggest that you explore an often-overlooked branch of the jewelry gift tree: charm bracelets and necklaces.

The initial outlay for the bracelet or necklace itself may seem a little steep, but think of it as an investment. The charms themselves are what make the package such an ideal gift. They are relatively inexpensive, offer a variety of options, and allow you to personalize your gift over and over again.

After, say, a memorable trip to Miami, you can buy a charm depicting the state of Florida. After playing couples softball together in a church league, you can buy a charm depicting a bat and ball.

Over time, the charm bracelet or necklace will tell the story of your relationship—much to the delight of your wife.

THE GIFT OF SELF

In some dialects of gift giving, you'll find there's an intangible present that sometimes speaks more loudly than a gift that can be held in one's hand. I call it the gift of self or the gift of presence. Being there when your spouse needs you speaks loudly to the one whose primary love language is gift giving. Sonia once said to me, "My husband loves softball more than he loves me."

"Why do you say that?" I inquired.

"On the day our baby was born, he played softball. I was lying in the hospital all afternoon while he played softball," she said.

"Was he there when the baby was born?"

"He stayed long enough for the baby to be born, but ten minutes afterward, he left. It was awful. It was such an important moment in our lives. I wanted us to share it together. I wanted Tony to be there with me."

That "baby" was now fifteen years old, and Sonia was talking about the event with all the emotion as though it had happened yesterday. I probed further. "Have you based your conclusion that Tony loves softball more than he loves you on this one experience?"

"No," she said. "On the day of my mother's funeral, he also played softball."

"Did he go to the funeral?"

"Yes, he did. He went to the funeral, but as soon as it was over, he left to get to his game. I couldn't believe it. My brothers and sisters came to the house with me, but my husband was playing softball."

Later, I asked Tony about those two events. He knew exactly what I was talking about. "I knew she would bring that up," he said. "I was there through all the labor and when the baby was born. I took pictures; I was so happy. I couldn't wait to tell the guys on the team, but my bubble was burst when I got back to the hospital that evening. She was furious with me. I couldn't believe what she was saying. I thought she would be proud of me for telling the team.

"And when her mother died? She probably didn't tell you that I took off work a week before she died and spent the whole week at the hospital and at her mother's house doing repairs and helping out. After she died and the funeral was over, I felt I had done all I could do. I needed a breather. I like to play softball, and I knew that would help me relax and relieve some of the stress I'd been under. I thought she would want me to take a break.

"I had done what I thought was important to her, but it wasn't enough. She has never let me forget those two days. She says that I love softball more than I love her. That's ridiculous."

He was a sincere husband who failed to understand the tremendous power of presence. In his wife's mind, his being there for her when she needed him was more important than anything else. **Physical presence in the time of crisis is the most powerful gift you can give if your spouse's primary love language is gift giving.** Your body becomes the symbol of your love. Remove the symbol, and the sense of love evaporates.

In counseling, Tony and Sonia worked through the hurts and misunderstandings of the past. Eventually, Sonia was able to forgive him, and Tony came to understand why his presence was so important to her.

You can avoid such heartache and years of resentment simply by reading your wife's verbal and nonverbal cues. If your wife says to you, "I really want you to be with me tonight/tomorrow/this afternoon," take her request seriously. From your perspective, the event may not seem important. Trust me, it is. And if you don't take it seriously—if you're less than responsive to her request—you may send a message to your wife without realizing it. A message you may regret for a long, long time.

Speak Up

If *your* primary love language is gift giving and the physical presence of your wife is important to *you*, your first order of business is to verbalize your feelings. Don't make her guess what's important to you. Spell it out. Give her a chance to speak your love language fluently.

The spirit of giving lies at the heart of love. All five love languages challenge us to give to our wives. However, for some people, gift giving—visible symbols of love—speaks the loudest.

IT'S A START

Let's say a guy recognizes the need for gifts in his relationship but has little or no experience as a gift giver. Perhaps he grew up in a low-income family where presents were rarely handed out. Perhaps he's never been much of a shopper—for himself or anyone else. Perhaps his own love language lies approximately 180 degrees from gift giving.

How might such a guy become fluent in a love language so foreign to him?

A good first step would be to make a list of all the gifts he can think of that got a big reaction from his wife. They may be presents he'd given her or presents given by other family members or friends. A list like that would give him an idea of the kind of gifts his wife would enjoy receiving. If he kept the list handy and added to it as often as possible, he could use it as a reference when it's time to shop.

If he's *seriously* worried about his gift-selecting prowess (or lack thereof), he could recruit the help of family members who know his wife well.

GIFT GIVING PHRASE BOOK

No one can be expected to master the love language of gift giving overnight. If you need a gift idea—and need it fast—try one of the following tried-and-true suggestions:

- The Twelve Days of Christmas are already established. But how about **twelve days of gifts** for your wedding anniversary, your wife's birthday, Mother's Day, or some other special occasion?

- Photos are inexpensive gifts that become more cherished as time passes. They can be even more special if you collect them for a while and then **present your wife with photo records** of the growth of your child, the life of your pet, the seasons of her flower garden, and more.

- Consider some good **"now and later" gifts**. For example, a bird feeder, a needlepoint kit, or seeds for a vegetable garden will yield rewards for a long time to come.

- Give your wife **"the gift of a day."** Sometime when you know she's free, take a day off and let her call all the shots for what she wants to do. (Or give her the entire day to herself.)

- Keep an eye open for **spontaneous, unexpected gifts**—from street flower vendors, roadside fruit or crafts dealers, or a favorite ice-cream shop on a hot day. Make sure they're all things she would appreciate.

- If she loves **gift shops or housewares stores**, let her browse without your grousing or getting restless.

- If she has a favorite game show or reality program, think of ways you might provide a personalized version just for her. If she loves home-design shows, for example, give her a budget and help from a friend, and let her **redesign one of the rooms** in your house.

- If you have an artistic bent, **create a rendering of her** in charcoal, watercolors, oils, clay, or some other medium.

- When she is approaching a milestone event (special birthday, anniversary), notify old friends of hers whom she hasn't heard from in a while. Request **simple, heartfelt gifts** (poems, bookmarks, prayers) for the special day. Keep them a secret until you present them to her at her big birthday bash.

- **Have a star registered** in your wife's name.

- **Buy stock in a company** your wife supports and let her follow the financial ups and downs over a period of time.

- **Give handmade coupons** for "services" your wife regularly requests, such as car washes, specific errands, and back rubs. Make sure to honor all coupons in a timely and cheerful manner.

- When money is tight, think of **appropriate symbolic gifts**. For example, instead of plane tickets, you might take your wife on a "flight of fancy" to daydream about what you would be doing together if money were no object. Or dig out videos of past vacations and relive special moments without leaving the comfort of your home.

- Offer your **"gift of presence"** during an especially hard time in her life—perhaps when she's visiting a very sick friend, caring for an elderly parent, or dealing with a job crisis.

- When your wife is away on a business trip, church retreat, or weekend getaway with her best friend, **hide a gift in her luggage**. Or arrange to have something delivered to her hotel room.

- **Add to the anticipation** of a big gift by offering vague clues as to what it is—perhaps in the form of jigsaw puzzle pieces that eventually create a picture of the gift.

ACTS OF SERVICE

5

How to Become Fluent in Acts of Service

(LOVE LANGUAGE #4)

Andre caught a glimpse of himself in the bathroom mirror and shook his head. *What a sight.* On his knees in front of a toilet. Rubber gloves pulled up to his elbows. A can of cleanser in one hand and a scrub brush in the other.

If the guys on his rugby team could see him now. Check that. If his *father* could see him now.

The old man was a firm believer in dividing household chores along gender lines. The husband mowed the lawn in the summer, shoveled snow in the winter, and fixed anything that was broken. The wife did everything else.

Suddenly Andre felt sorry for his dad. The old man probably never experienced the payoff that comes from completing a surprise act of service for his wife. Andre grinned as he thought about his own wife's reaction to *his* latest surprise act.

She would come home to find not just a spotless bathroom but a new shower curtain, rug, towel set, and toilet-paper holder—the very ones she'd pointed out to him in a catalog (and then mistakenly assumed he'd forgotten about).

She'd scream, of course. Hold her hand over her mouth in amazement. Notice and comment on every little detail, right down to the toothbrush holder that was no longer gunked-up with dried toothpaste. Laugh in embarrassment as tears roll down her cheeks. Wrap her arms around him for a long, sensual hug. Whisper in his ear how lucky she is to be married to such a caring, thoughtful, surprising . . . *attractive* man.

Suddenly Andre felt sorry for anyone who wasn't him.

A HARD-EARNED HAPPILY EVER AFTER

You might conclude that Andre and his wife are a match made in love language heaven. And you'd be right . . . though it wasn't always that way. Andre didn't telepathically pick up on his wife's fondness for acts of service the first time they met. He wasn't some linguistic savant who started speaking her love language fluently right away.

Andre and his wife endured years of doubt, frustration, annoyance, and confusion as they struggled to make their relationship work, to make their needs known to each other, and to find ways to meet those needs. In their darkest hours, they questioned whether they were really meant to be together.

Even after Andre discovered his wife's love language, he struggled with learning acts of service. He argued that the things he was *already* doing—putting gas in the car, taking out the trash, bringing home the lion's share of their household income—should count as acts of service. He expected his wife to feel loved based on those things. In essence, he wanted her to change *her* needs to fit *his* solutions. It took awhile for him to figure out—and then come to grips with—the kinds of acts that meant most to her.

Cleaning the bathroom, for one.

His progress was slow but steady. With practice (and more than a little trial and error), Andre eventually became fluent in acts of service—and you can too. In fact, we can break down the fluency strategy into three easy-to-remember parts:

Impact

Initiative

Attitude

If any one of these elements is missing or off-kilter, your attempts to communicate love to your wife through acts of service will be thwarted.

Let's look first at the importance of Impact.

DEEP IMPACT

I've got some good news and some bad news for you.

The bad news is, you could spend an entire long weekend doing chores—raking leaves, preparing your lawn for winter, winding up hoses and putting them away, winterizing your cars, pulling Thanksgiving and Christmas decorations from the attic, putting weather strips on your windows and sliding doors, tuning up your snowblower, cutting logs for the fireplace— and not add a drop to your wife's love tank.

> **Making an impact on your wife means working smarter, not harder.**

The good news is, you could bring home Chinese takeout, clean the kitchen afterward, and then put the kids to bed by yourself on a night when she's facing a deadline at work (or is just wiped out after a long day)—and *overflow* that very same love tank!

When it comes to acts of service, you're not judged by the amount of time you put in or even by how hard you work. You're judged by your effectiveness—the impact you have.

A starting pitcher in baseball may work on his delivery constantly, making sure the release point of his off-speed pitches matches that of his fastball. He may take hundreds of extra ground balls and line drives after practice in a quest to field his position better. He may study hours of film every night, learning the tendencies of various batters and baserunners.

In the end, though, he's judged by one criterion: Does he get batters out? If the answer is no, none of his other work makes much of a difference. What matters is whether he's effective where it counts.

Andre didn't make that connection at first. He worked hard—at the wrong tasks. And he failed to make a dent in his wife's love-language needs.

For someone who takes pride in his work, that can be a tough pill to swallow. Most of us are wired with an instinctive desire to prove our worth—as husbands, providers, and caretakers. Beyond that, we want our work to *mean* something. And we want credit for the things we do.

The Way Things Used to Be

Many people get married believing their spouse is already fluent in acts of service. They base their belief on the way the spouse acted while they were dating. Many of these people quickly discover that what two people do for each other before marriage is no indication of what they'll do after marriage.

The process of falling in love can effect odd changes in our behavior and cause us to do things completely out of character. After marriage, we revert to being the people we were before we fell in love. That's when learning a new love language becomes necessary.

In order to become fluent in acts of service, we need to kick that mindset to the curb. We need to let our wife guide us in determining what is and isn't an effective act. We need to let her instruct us on how to make an impact.

What does love look like to your wife?

What actions make her feel genuinely and spectacularly loved?

The answer to these questions will guide your actions. Depending on her personality—and your relationship history—she may or may not feel comfortable sharing the answers with you. You may need to put her at ease, to help her recognize your genuine desire to meet her acts of service needs.

One way to do that is to invite her to compile her "Ultimate Honeydew (or Honey Do) List"—the four or five acts of service that would mean the most to her. Her list might include a household chore she absolutely despises, an idea for taking some pressure off her, a way for her to free up some time for herself, a project that she's dreamed of for years, or other service suggestions.

Whatever makes your wife feel genuinely and spectacularly loved is where your focus and effort should go.

The list doesn't need to be comprehensive. It's just a starting point—a snapshot of your wife's current emotional-needs landscape. Once you have it, though, treat it like the valuable resource it is.

HOW DO YOU SAY "ASAP" IN ACTS OF SERVICE?

The transition from receiving your wife's to-do list to breaking ground on your first official act of service is critical. Think of it as a baton hand-off in a 4 x 100-meter relay or a pit stop in the Indianapolis 500. Speed and execution are everything.

Call it . . . initiative. Taking the fight *to* your wife's list instead of letting it come to you.

You may have every intention of tackling the items on her list—when you have the time, opportunity, and energy to do so. But in relationships, as in business, sports, and just about any other walk of life, good intentions will get you only so far. In order to make them count, you have to turn those good intentions into something tangible, something appreciable.

Whatever goodwill you build up by encouraging your wife to share her ultimate to-do list with you will be squandered in no time if that list gets buried under a mountain of paperwork on your desk. The last thing you want is for your wife to have to remind you of the things you intended to do for her.

That won't feel like love to her. Love is always freely given. It can't be demanded, cajoled, or coaxed from someone.

That's why it's vital that you take the initiative in completing an act of service on your wife's list as soon as you possibly can. In doing so, you demonstrate your future intentions and give her a sense of just how important her emotional well-being is to you.

The most logical thing to do is choose the easiest item on the list and complete that. And if time is of the essence, there's nothing wrong with taking that route. If time is *not* a factor, however—if you have the resources and wherewithal to do something bigger and bolder—your absolute best strategy is to tackle the item on the list that will mean the most to her. The one closest to her heart.

Take on the task, and get it done—and done well. Show your wife good *results* instead of good intentions. When the first item is finished, turn your attention to the rest of the list.

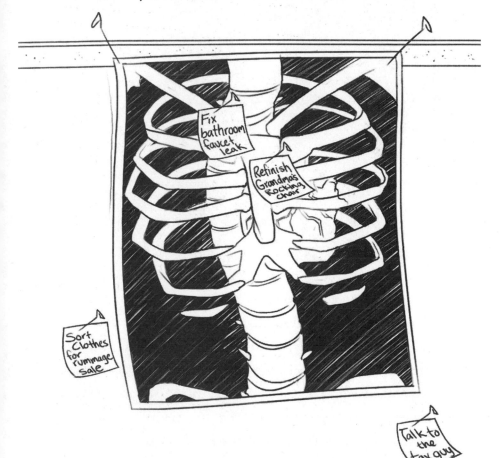

Easier said than done, right? Especially with so many other things vying for your time, attention, and energy. The key to initiating acts of service is to make it a "3-D experience" with Drive, Discipline, and Dedication.

Drive speaks to your motivation. To keep the *reason* for your acts of service fresh in your mind, tape your favorite picture of your wife, along with her to-do list, on your bathroom mirror or someplace else where you'll see it every day. Every time you look at the photo, think of how you can show love to the woman in it through an act of service—whether it's an idea from her list or a surprise that you know she'll appreciate.

Discipline refers to the scheduling and prioritizing necessary to accomplish some of the more ambitious projects on the list. Six large garden boxes aren't built, set up, and filled in a day. A custom closet organizer can't be installed in an hour or two after work. Some acts of service are going to cut into your already-busy schedule. Some may require you to postpone—or sacrifice—your own chores or pastimes.

Dedication is making sure that what's started gets finished. Dedication is staying committed to an act of service until it can be presented as a token of love. Dedication is what prevents would-be demonstrations of affection from becoming partially completed reminders of more pressing priorities.

Remember, every delay or aborted attempt to complete an act of service sends a clear message to your wife: *this isn't important to me.*

SERVICE WITH A SMILE

Just as crucial as the actual act of service itself is the *attitude* with which you perform it. In fact, the right thing done with the wrong attitude can actually cause more harm than good. If your wife senses resentment or irritation in you while you're performing an act of service for her, she won't feel affirmed. She'll feel like an imposition, a bother, a drain on your time and energy.

Where's the love in that?

For maximum impact, **your acts of service should be done with eagerness,** an excitement to do something meaningful for your wife. **They should be done with good humor,** even the ones that take you way, way, *way* out of your comfort zone. And **they should be done with humility.** Don't call attention to yourself while you're performing them. Don't make a big deal about them afterward. Refuse to play the hero card or the martyr card. Remember who you're doing them for and why.

If Acts of Service Is Your Primary Love Language . . .

Keep in mind that love is a choice and cannot be coerced. You can't use criticism or demands to get what you need. With enough bullying, you may get acquiescence from your wife.

She may do what you want, but it will certainly not be an expression of love.

A better option is to give guidance by making requests: "I wish you would keep the house picked up, sort the mail, phone my mother more often." But you cannot create or demand the will to love. Each of us must decide daily to love or not to love our wives.

THE DOORMAT CONUNDRUM

Of the five love languages, acts of service seems to have the most potential for abuse—or at least the perception of abuse. A wife with less-than-noble intentions could conceivably convince her husband to do just about anything for her, all in the name of love.

One fed-up wife put it this way: "I have served him for twenty years. I have waited on him hand and foot. I have been his doormat while he ignored me, mistreated me, and humiliated me in front of my friends and family. I don't hate him. I wish him no ill, but I resent him, and I no longer wish to live with him."

For two decades that woman performed acts of service for her husband. But they weren't expressions of love. They were done out of fear, guilt, and resentment. How many other well-meaning men and women have similar stories? How many of them are former (or current) members of the Doormat Society?

A doormat is an inanimate object, something you step on, wipe your feet on, and kick around occasionally. It has no will of its own. It doesn't object to the way it's treated. It serves its purpose. Period.

When we treat our wives as objects—or even give them cause to feel as though they're being treated as objects—we eliminate the possibility of love. Manipulation by guilt ("If you were a good wife, you would do this for me") is not the language of love. Coercion by fear ("You will do this or you will be sorry") is alien to love.

Likewise, when a husband's genuine efforts to speak love through acts of service are regularly met with dissatisfaction or indifference by his wife, a reevaluation may be in order.

As we mentioned earlier, becoming fluent in a second love language takes time. Mistakes are inevitable. Not every idea will work, especially if the two of you aren't yet on the same page.

If, on other hand, you perform the acts of service that your wife said mean the most to her, and you consistently get criticism—or no reaction at all—from her, it's a pretty safe bet that acts of service isn't your wife's love language after all.

ACTS OF SERVICE PHRASE BOOK

You've committed yourself to becoming fluent in acts of service so that you can express love to your wife. Good for you. As a nonnative speaker, you'll find there are times when you're stuck for inspiration. Here are some ideas to get you unstuck.

■ Many men know of a chore (or chores) that their wife has already given up hope of ever seeing done. **Surprise her—and get the job done**.

■ **If she asks you to do something, do it**. Don't make her repeat herself.

■ Plan to get up a half hour earlier (or stay up a half hour later) each day for a week, and use that time to **plan and perform acts of service for your wife**.

■ **Think of something she would never expect**. Take the dog to the groomer, reorganize the basement to make room for her home business files, clean out the pantry and kitchen cabinets.

■ **Make dinner**. Really cook it, and don't forget the vegetables. Then clean up, and don't forget to wipe the stove.

■ **Take your wife "shopping" in the Yellow Pages or online**. Let her pick out a needed service, whether it's gutter cleaning, painting, or carpet steaming.

■ **Think of your wife's most frequent complaints**, and go overboard in preventing them again in the near future.

■ **Make yourself accessible to her in times of extended grief** (such as the death of a parent or pet). Supporting her during tough times can be a great act of service.

- Don't always announce what you do for your wife. Occasionally **perform a covert act of service without saying anything**, and see how long it takes her to notice.

- If your wife always seems rushed in the mornings, **find a way to give her a few more minutes.** Take an earlier (or later) shift in the bathroom. Pack the kids' lunches. Get the coffee ready.

- **Make a list of the skills and abilities your friends possess**. Which ones can you call on to perform an act of service for your wife that you're incapable of doing?

- If your wife enjoys what you do for her so much that she wants to get in on the fun, **work together to perform acts of service** for other people you know. (Before you know it, you'll find that you are spending quality time together while you plan.)

- **Consider how you might serve someone** (or something) your wife loves, whether it's a friend, a family member, a fellow churchgoer, or a favorite cause.

- **Run interference for your wife** during one of her favorite TV shows. Take care of all the phone calls, kid emergencies, and so on.

- If you know of other men reading this book, exchange ideas with them to **come up with new, workable relationship strategies**.

PHYSICAL TOUCH

6

How to Become Fluent in Physical Touch

(LOVE LANGUAGE #5)

As a kid, how often did you:

Play touch football in your neighborhood?

Arm wrestle your dad?

Thumb wrestle your brother?

Play tag at recess?

Dole out noogies, wet willies, wrist burns, and Hertz Donuts?

Play Marco Polo in a swimming pool?

For many guys, physical touch is a huge part of growing up. Left to their own devices, **boys can make a contact sport out of any game, activity, or car ride.**

As we get older, we're taught to respect other people's personal space and keep our hands to ourselves. Aside from handshakes, high fives, and the occasional side hug, our interpersonal interaction as adults is largely contact-free. We touch no one, and no one touches us.

Sometimes that hands-off approach extends to marriage too.

After the honeymoon period, when the newlyweds can't get enough of each other, many couples settle into a pattern of ever-increasing physical distance. The demands of a busy world—as well as any number of emotional issues—conspire to keep husband and wife at arm's length from each other.

For roughly four-fifths of married people, that distance may not seem like a glaring problem. (That number assumes a relatively equal distribution of primary love languages among the general population.) Their love tanks are filled by words of affirmation, quality time, gift giving, or acts of service. They may enjoy physical touch, but they don't *need* it to feel loved and cared for. Their emotional well-being isn't tied to it.

This chapter is dedicated to the *other* 20 percent—the spouses whose primary love language is physical touch.

THE TOUCHABLES

If you or your wife is a foodie, chances are you've heard of "supertasters," people whose sense of taste is so acute that they experience food differently than most other people do. For a supertaster, sugar is sweeter, sodium is saltier, fat is creamier, and bitterness is unbearable. Some supertasters can detect even the slightest differences in the fat content of milk and other foods.

The jury is out as to whether supertasting abilities are a blessing or a curse. On the plus side, with their enhanced taste buds, supertasters can isolate and enjoy the many ingredients that go into their favorite foods. Supertasters make excellent food critics. On the minus side, supertasters are repulsed by certain foods—including healthy dark green vegetables—that other people enjoy.

If your wife's primary love language is physical touch, think of her

as a "supertoucher." She can sense love and affection—among other things—in the slightest arm squeeze or back caress. **Physical contact that wouldn't even register with most people has the potential to thrill her, change her mood, brighten her day, and—most importantly—make her feel loved and cared for.**

The intensity of her tactile experience plays a large role in her relationships. The closer she is to someone, whether it's a friend or family member, the more she enjoys physical touch with that person—a bear hug with her brother, a kiss on the cheek from her mother, an arm around her shoulder from her best friend. Likewise, the *withholding* of physical touch by those closest to her has the potential to cause her more pain and anxiety than most nonnative speakers of her love language can imagine.

From her perspective, physical touch can make or break a relationship. It can communicate love or hate. A slap in the face is shocking to anyone, but it would be devastating to someone whose primary love language is physical touch. A tender hug communicates love and affection to most people, but it *shouts* love to those who speak physical touch.

The thought process of such a person goes like this: *Whatever there is of me resides in my body. To touch my body is to touch me. To withdraw from my body is to distance yourself from me emotionally.*

Even people who speak other love languages can understand that thinking to a certain degree. Whether we realize it or not, most of us adhere to certain physical touch expectations in our culture. To deviate from them is to invite scrutiny and misunderstanding. How many times a week do you shake hands with clients, fellow church members, golf partners, and casual acquaintances? In our culture, shaking hands is a way of communicating openness and friendliness to another person. If you extend your hand to someone and he leaves you hanging by refusing to shake it, you'll likely assume one of three things:

The guy is a raging jerk.

He has no interest in getting to know you.

Things are not right in your relationship.

Your reaction to the snub will depend on who's doing the snubbing. If it's an opponent you just beat in a pickup basketball game, you probably won't give it a second thought. If it's your boss, you may start to panic, wondering what you've done wrong and when the hammer's going to drop.

And so it goes for the wife who speaks physical touch as a primary love language. **When that touch isn't forthcoming, she takes it personally.** She may lose self-esteem. She may worry about the state of her friendships and relationships. She may feel lonely, even when she's surrounded by friends and loved ones.

As her husband, her primary source of love and affirmation, the responsibility for giving her the physical touch she desires is yours. **Some might call that pressure. You can choose to look at it as a challenge—and an opportunity.**

TAKING STOCK

If your kids (or your friends' kids or your nieces or nephews) play high school sports, you may be familiar with baseline concussion tests. If not, here's how they work. Before the season starts, the athlete takes a computer-based test that measures reaction time, memory capacity, speed of mental processing, and executive functioning of the brain. The test serves as a document of how the athlete's brain works when it's healthy.

If the athlete suffers a concussion during the season, doctors can then readminister the test and compare the new results with the baseline test. That point of comparison allows them to determine where damage has been done so they can plan their treatment accordingly.

That same principle—in reverse—can be applied to learning your wife's love language. If you're serious about becoming fluent in physical touch, you may want to consider conducting a "baseline test" of your current physical touch relationship with your wife.

At the end of a typical weekday, after your wife has gone to bed, do a mental review of your physical interaction with her that day. Write down every time you kissed her

gave her a hug

held her hand

put your arm around her

initiated foot-to-foot contact under the table

grabbed her around the waist

gave her a high five

playfully wrestled with her

rubbed her shoulder

stroked her hair

caressed her back

had any other meaningful, purposeful, affectionate physical contact with her.

Be as precise and comprehensive as you can in compiling your list. Resist the urge to inflate the numbers to make yourself look better. Remember, you're just looking for baseline figures—points of comparison to use later. Besides, there's no reason for anyone but you to see your list.

Once you have a fairly concrete idea of how much physical touch you provide your wife on a given day, you can begin looking for areas in which you can do better. For example, if you find there are one or two types of touches that you go to over and over again, you might look at some other types of touches that are underrepresented on your list and consider trying them more often. Crunch your numbers, set your goals, and plan your strategy.

Once your strategy is in place, mark some dates in your calendar for additional self-evaluations to check your progress. Compare them to your baseline figures to see where you're improving and where you need more improvement.

NICE TOUCH

Anatomically speaking, physical touch may be the easiest love language of all to begin learning. The human body was designed with touch receptors throughout. You could touch your wife lovingly almost anywhere on her body.

Theoretically.

In reality, **not all touches are created equal**. Some will bring more pleasure to her than others. Your best instructor is the one being touched, of course—in this case, your wife. After all, she's the one you're seeking to love. She knows best what she perceives as a loving touch. **Don't insist on touching her in *your* way and in *your* time.** Learn to speak her love dialect.

Like it or not, your wife may find some touches uncomfortable or irritating. To continue using those touches is to communicate the opposite of love—to suggest that you're not sensitive to her needs and that you care little about her perceptions of what's pleasant. **The fact that a certain kind of touch brings pleasure to you doesn't mean it will— or should—bring pleasure to your wife.**

> The only touches available to you are the ones that bring pleasure to your wife.

Some love touches are explicit and demand your full attention. Sexual foreplay and intercourse would certainly fall into this category (more on these later). A sensual back rub would also qualify. Explicit love touches usually involve more time and effort on your part—not only where the actual touching is concerned but also in preparing and understanding how to communicate love to your wife in that way. **If a back massage communicates love loudly to your wife, then any time, money, and energy you spend in learning to be a good masseur will be well invested.**

Other love touches are implicit and require only a moment. These would include putting your hand on your wife's shoulder as you pour her a cup of coffee or rubbing your body against hers as you pass in the kitchen.

Implicit love touches require little time but much thought—especially if physical touch is not your primary love language and if you didn't grow up in a "touching family." Sitting close to each other as you watch your favorite TV shows requires no additional time, but it may communicate your love loudly. Touching your wife as you walk through the room where she's sitting takes only a moment. Touching each other when you leave the house and again when you return may involve only a brief kiss or hug, but it will speak volumes to your wife.

Once you discover that physical touch is the primary love language of your wife, you are limited only by your imagination when it comes to expressing love. Brainstorming new ways and places to touch can be an exciting challenge.

If you've never been an under-the-table toucher in the past, you may find that secretive contact adds a spark to your dining out.

If you're not accustomed to holding hands in public, you may find that you can fill your wife's emotional love tank simply by strolling through a parking lot hand in hand.

If you don't normally kiss as soon as you get into the car together, you may find that it greatly enhances your travels.

Hugging your wife before she goes shopping not only expresses love but it may bring her home sooner.

Try new touches in new places and let your wife give you feedback on whether she finds it pleasurable. Remember, she has the final word. You are learning to speak her love language.

A CATEGORY UNTO ITSELF

Surely a red-blooded, testosterone-driven man can be forgiven for smiling slyly when he discovers that his wife experiences love primarily through physical touch. That's like hitting the love-language lottery, isn't it? After all, physical touch *does* include sex, right? Right?

Perhaps.

Not necessarily.

It depends on your wife.

Some wives may indeed find emotional fulfillment from the physical intimacy of lovemaking. Other wives may put sex in a separate category from other kinds of physical touch. Either way, it's important to remember whose needs are in focus here.

The purpose of becoming fluent in the language of physical touch is not to get your own desires met but to make your wife feel genuinely loved and cared for. If she senses that your efforts at physical touch are merely preludes to sex—ways to "get her in the mood"—she may start to resent them. And in the process, you'll lose some credibility.

Your wife needs to know that your aim is true, your intentions are noble, and your efforts are directed at her. If that means removing sex from the love language equation, so be it. The two of you can address your physical intimacy in another setting.

> **Physical Touch is not code for foreplay.**

There are three points we must reiterate in the context of physical touch and sex. The first involves appropriate and inappropriate touching. Remember, **it's your wife who draws the line**. If she's uncomfortable with touching that borders on groping, she should feel free to tell you so. That way, you can adjust your actions accordingly. Her feelings must be respected.

Second, the fact that your wife's reaction to physical touch is so fraught with meaning means that **any betrayal in that area will be devastating to her**—more so than it might be for someone else. Marriage counselors' files are filled with records of husbands and wives who are grappling with the emotional trauma of an unfaithful spouse. That trauma, however, is compounded for the individual whose primary love language is physical touch. The idea of the love for which she longs being given to another person is almost too much to bear. Her emotional love tank is not only drained; it is exploded. Only massive repairs can fix the damage.

Third, **if sexual intercourse is indeed your wife's primary dialect, nothing should stop you from becoming the best lover you can possibly be for her.** The more you read about and discuss the art of sexual lovemaking, the more you will improve your ability to express love in that way.

WHEN IT'S NEEDED MOST

If physical touch is important under normal circumstances, it is absolutely essential in times of crisis. Even people who don't speak physical touch as their primary love language almost instinctively cling to one another in times of emergency, loss, and upheaval. The more serious the situation, the more likely we are to hug or clasp hands.

That's a testament to the power of physical touch to communicate love. In a time of crisis, more than anything, we need to feel loved. We cannot always change events, but we can survive if we feel loved.

All marriages will experience crises. Some can be anticipated; others can't. The death of parents is inevitable. Automobile accidents injure and kill thousands every year. Disease is no respecter of persons. Disappointments are a part of life. The most important thing you can do for your wife in a time of crisis is to love her. If her primary love language is physical touch, nothing is more important than holding her as she cries. Your words may mean little, but your physical touch will communicate that you care.

A crisis provides a unique opportunity for expressing love. It's vital that you seize that opportunity. Your tender touches will be remembered long after the crisis has passed. Your failure to touch may never be forgotten.

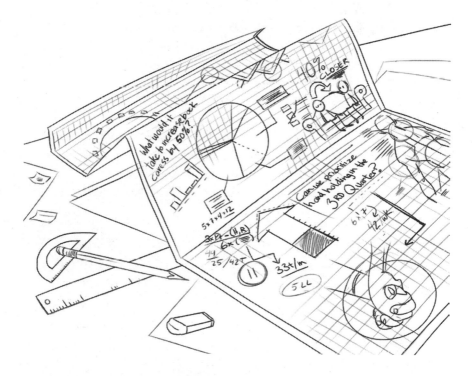

PHYSICAL TOUCH PHRASE BOOK

Think of this as a starter's kit—or an emergency resource—for communicating in the love language of physical touch. If you're stuck for an idea of how to show tactile love to your wife, try one of these suggestions:

- **Make touching your wife a normal part of your routine**. Run your fingers through her hair while she's reading. Touch her shoulder as she works in the kitchen. Even the smallest acts can build intimacy over time.

- **Make a point of hugging and kissing your wife** when you say goodbye in the morning, when you come home in the evening, and before you go to bed at night. It's easy to let these rituals slide, particularly when you've been married for a while.

- Change your usual patterns and routines to **encourage more physical contact between you and your wife**. If each of you has a special chair, move them to within arm's length of each other. Switch sides of the bed. The awkwardness of the new arrangement is likely to lead to unexpected touching opportunities.

- If the two of you normally sit across from each other in a restaurant, next time get a booth and **sit side by side**. If you usually sit side by side, next time sit across from each other and engage in a little foot play under the table.

- Set aside an evening for some touch experiments to **determine where your wife most likes to be touched**. As you move from spot to spot, ask her to give you a thumbs-up, a thumbs-down, or an indifferent thumb sideways to indicate her reaction. Make a mental note of the spots that get a thumbs-up.

- Check out websites, DVDs, and books that teach **various techniques of body massage**. Experiment to see which methods your wife enjoys most.

- Think back to your early dates and **recall the thrill of physical touch** that perhaps you now take for granted. The next time you're alone with your wife, try to rekindle some of that original excitement.

- The next time you shop for your wife, **look for things that will appeal to her tactile nature**—things that are pleasant to touch, such as a cashmere sweater, a plush throw pillow, or warm, fuzzy slippers.

- The next time she's sick, remember **the healing power of touch**. When her head hurts, offer to rub her neck and temples. When she's suffering from a cold or flu, frequently rub her forehead.

- If you have kids, train them to show love for Mom through physical touch. Make it a tradition in your household for the family to hold hands during prayer. **Encourage your children to be generous with their hugs**. The more often you model physically affirming behavior toward your wife, the more likely it is your kids will follow your example.

- For a designated period of time, **communicate with your wife using only physical touch**. Don't say anything as you shower her with physical attention.

- When she's facing away from you in bed, **write short messages on her back** and see if she can tell what you're writing. (FYI: "I adore you" will get a much better reaction than "Time to vacuum.")

7

What Languages Do You Speak?

M aybe you had an aha moment the first time you glanced at a list of the five love languages. Maybe you read the chapter on words of affirmation or acts of service and said, "Bingo! That's me!" or "That's *definitely* my wife."

Then again, maybe it *didn't* happen that way.

For many people, discovering a primary love language—your spouse's or your own—is a challenge. The clues aren't always as obvious as we might hope. We shouldn't be surprised. We are, after all, complex individuals. We have a variety of interests. We respond to all kinds of stimuli. There's no reason people *should* expect to figure us out quickly.

As a result of that complexity, many couples operate under false assumptions when it comes to love languages. How many wives have drawers full of jewelry, stuffed animals, frilly lingerie, and other gifts that their husbands were sure would make them feel loved? How many husbands cringe in embarrassment at the memory of words of affirmation that fell flat? How many spouses still harbor resentment over acts of service that went unnoticed? How many of them "appreciate" what their spouses are trying to do but secretly wish for a little *less* quality time or physical touch?

THE OFFICIAL LOVE LANGUAGE OF MEN?

Likewise, how many well-meaning people have fooled themselves— and their spouses—when it comes to their *own* love language? Guys are especially susceptible to self-deception in this area for one simple reason.

S-E-X.

Most guys would admit to enjoying sex—a lot. So much so, in fact, that they assume physical touch is their primary love language and sexual intercourse is their dialect. That's sound logic, isn't it?

Not necessarily.

As you no doubt remember from health class, sexual desire in males is physically based. The desire for sexual intercourse is stimulated by the buildup of seminal fluid in the seminal vesicles. When the seminal vesicles are full, there is a physical push for release. Thus, the male's desire for sexual intercourse has a physical root. It's not necessarily related to his love language.

If you're uncertain as to whether physical touch is your primary love language, consider whether you enjoy hands-on contact outside the bedroom. Are you energized by hand-holding, back rubs, and affectionate caresses? If not, physical touch may not be your love language.

Sexual desire is quite different from the emotional need to feel loved. That doesn't mean sexual intercourse is unimportant to the person who speaks a love language other than physical touch. It's *extremely* important. But sexual intercourse alone will not meet a husband's need to feel loved. His wife must speak his primary emotional love language as well.

When his wife speaks his primary love language and his emotional love tank is full, and he speaks her primary love language and her emotional tank is full, the sexual aspect of their relationship will likely take care of itself. Most sexual problems in marriage have little to do with physical technique but everything to do with meeting emotional needs.

KNOW THYSELF

So what *is* your primary love language? What makes you feel most loved by your wife? What do you desire above all else? If the answer to those questions doesn't leap to your mind immediately, try a different approach.

Think about the *negative* use of love languages. What does your wife do or say—or *fail* to do or say—that hurts you deeply? Your answers will be instructive. If, for example, your deepest pain is caused by the critical, judgmental words of your wife, then your primary love language may be words of affirmation.

Makes sense, right? If your primary love language is used negatively by your wife—that is, if she does the opposite of what you desire—it will hurt you more deeply than it would hurt someone else. Not only is she neglecting to speak your primary love language but she's actually using that language as a weapon against you.

WORDS OF AFFIRMATION

"If she ever gave me a real compliment, I'd probably die of shock."

If it grieves you deeply that your wife seldom gives you a gift for any occasion, then perhaps your primary love language is gift giving. If your deepest hurt is that your wife seldom gives you quality time, then it seems reasonable to assume that quality time is your primary love language.

QUALITY TIME

"It seems like she has time for everyone but me."

Another approach to discovering your primary love language is to look back over your marriage and ask, "What have I most often requested of my wife?" The answer will likely reveal your primary love language. Though your requests may occasionally have been interpreted as nagging by your wife, they are, in fact, your efforts to secure emotional love from her. Likewise, your wife's most frequent request to you probably indicates her primary love language.

ACTS OF SERVICE

"Why am I the only one who cares how clean the kitchen is?"

Yet another way to discover your primary love language is to examine what *you* do or say to express love to your wife. Chances are, what you're doing for her is what you wish she would do for you. If you're constantly doing acts of service for your wife, perhaps (though not always) that is *your* love language. If words of affirmation speak love to you, chances are you'll use them in speaking love to your wife. Thus, you may discover your

GIFT GIVING

"She went to Washington DC, and I didn't even get a lousy Nationals T-shirt?"

own primary love language by asking, "How do *I* consciously express my love to my wife?"

PHYSICAL TOUCH
"Do I have some kind of skin disease or something?"

This approach will yield only a potential *clue* to your love language. It is not an absolute indicator. For example, the husband who learned from his father to show love to his wife by giving her nice gifts expresses his love to his wife by doing what his father did. Yet gift giving is not his primary love language. He's simply doing what he was trained to do by his father.

Speak for Yourself

"Whenever I look back over the last ten years of my marriage and ask myself what I have most requested of Peter, my love language becomes obvious. I have requested quality time most often. Over and over again, I have asked him if we could go on a picnic, take a weekend together away, shut the TV off for just an hour and talk with each other, take a walk together, and on and on. I have felt neglected and unloved because seldom did he ever respond to my request. He gave me nice gifts for my birthday and special occasions and wondered why I wasn't excited about them."

—**Elizabeth**

Follow the Sound of the Criticism

Spouses tend to criticize each other most loudly in the areas where they themselves have the deepest emotional need. Their criticism is an ineffective way of pleading for love. If we understand that, it may help us process criticism in a more productive manner.

You may say to your wife after she gives you a criticism, "It sounds like that's extremely important to you. Could you explain why it's so crucial?" Criticism often needs clarification. Initiating such a conversation may eventually turn the criticism into a request rather than a demand.

Let's say Kristina criticizes her husband, Jeff, for hunting, which happens to be his favorite pastime. She knows it relaxes him and gives him a much-needed opportunity to spend time outdoors—and with his friends. Yet she complains about it every chance she gets. She exaggerates the amount of time he actually spends hunting and says he never spends that kind of time on her.

In reality, her criticism may not be an expression of her hatred for hunting. Instead, she may be blaming hunting as the thing that keeps Jeff from vacuuming the house, or mowing the grass. When Jeff learns to meet her need for love by speaking her emotional love language (acts of service), Kristina will likely start to support him in his passion for hunting.

TOO CLOSE TO CALL

If two love languages seem to be equal for you—that is, if both speak loudly to you—then perhaps you are bilingual. If so, you make things much easier for your wife. You give her two options for filling your love tank, either of which will strongly communicate affection to you.

If you'd prefer to break an apparent tie—or get a more definitive take on your primary love language—you may wish to take the 5 Love Languages Profile found toward the back of the book. Consider your answers carefully. When you're finished, discuss your results with your wife. Get her input. Does she recognize that love language in you?

Then have her take the profile too!

If the profile fails to reveal a definitive answer, don't give up. I've found that two kinds of people may have difficulty discovering their primary love language. The first is the individual whose emotional love tank has been full for a long time. His wife has expressed love to him in so many different ways, he's not sure which of those ways makes him feel most loved. Poor guy. We should all have such problems.

The second is the individual whose love tank has been empty for so long that he doesn't remember what makes him feel loved. The circumstances that lead to such a pitiful state of affairs will vary from person to person. However, what these people have in common is the assurance that their condition need not be permanent. Love languages don't disappear; they simply lie dormant, waiting to be rediscovered.

The best way to rediscover your love language is to recall your experience of falling in love and ask yourself, "What did I like about my wife in those days? What did she do or say that made me desire to be with her?" If you can conjure up those memories, you will get some idea as to your primary love language.

With that in mind, let me suggest also that you spend some time writing down what you think is your primary love language. Then list the other four love languages in order of importance. Also write down what you think is the primary love language of your wife. (You may also list the other four in order of importance if you wish.) Ask your wife to do the same. Sit down together and discuss what you guessed to be each other's primary love language. Then reveal what you consider to be your own primary love language.

One of the best ways to confirm your findings is to play a game with your wife called Tank Check.

THE TANK CHECK GAME

NUMBER OF PLAYERS: Two (you and your wife)

FREQUENCY: Play three times a week for three weeks

HOW TO PLAY: When you are both home in the evening, your wife starts the game by asking, "On a scale of zero to ten, how is your love tank tonight?" Zero means empty; ten means, "I am full of love and can't handle any more." You give a reading on your emotional love tank: 10, 9, 8, 7, 6, 5, 4, 3, 2, 1, or 0, indicating how full it is.

Your wife asks, "What can I do to help fill it?" Then you make a suggestion—something you would like your wife to do or say that evening. To the best of her ability, she will respond to your request.

Then you ask your wife the same questions so that both of you have the opportunity to do readings on your love tanks and make suggestions toward filling them.

If you play the game for three weeks, you will be hooked on it, and it can become a playful way of stimulating love expressions in your marriage.

WHERE DO WE GO FROM HERE?

As we mentioned earlier in the book, most people marry someone whose primary love language is different from theirs. If that's the case with you and your wife, spend some time talking about your differences.

Let's say your primary love language is physical touch and your wife's is quality time. What does that mean? Start your discussion at the most practical level. For one thing, it means your wife would feel most comfortable showing you love by hanging out with you, doing the

things you do. And it means you would feel most comfortable showing love to your wife through kisses, hugs, caresses, and back rubs.

Freeze the discussion there for a moment.

You've talked about what would be *comfortable* for you both. Unfortunately, what's comfortable for each of you won't impact the other. In order to become fluent in your wife's love language, you must step out of your comfort zone. And your wife must do the same for you.

To take those steps—to put your wife's needs ahead of your own comfort—is an act of love in itself. You're showing your wife that you're willing to do whatever it takes to make your relationship better and stronger—and to make your wife feel spectacularly loved.

It's vital that you keep those sacrifices—that willingness to step outside your comfort zones—in mind whenever you feel annoyed or frustrated with your wife's attempts to communicate via your love language. Remember, it isn't her native tongue. She's ventured outside her comfort zone for you.

Appreciation and gratitude must be shown.

It may not always be pretty. It may not always be effective. But it is genuine.

The more leeway and understanding you give each other as you try to learn each other's love language, the more success you'll have.

At a Glance: Discovering Your Love Language

If you don't have time to read the entire chapter right now, here's the key info you need—in ultracondensed form. To identify your primary love language, ask yourself three questions:

1. What does your wife do or fail to do that hurts you most deeply? The opposite of what hurts you most is probably your love language.
2. What have you most often requested of your wife? That is likely the thing that would make you feel most loved.
3. In what way do you regularly express love to your wife? Your method of expressing love may be the method that would also make you feel loved.

8

Troubleshooting

In an ideal world, a couple would discover each other's love language on their very first date. Then, as their relationship grew, so would their communication and appreciation for each other. Their efforts to become fluent would coincide with their falling in love. By the time they got married, both of them would be bilingual in love languages.

As you may have noticed, we don't live in an ideal world. We live in a world where the New York Yankees can capture twenty-seven world championships in eighty-six years, and the Chicago Cubs can go over a hundred years without winning *one*.

Baseball aside, the reality for many couples is that they allow their feelings of romance, excitement, and "in-loveness" to carry them into marriage before they've had a chance to consider each other's love language. From there, the busyness and pressures of everyday life leave them little time or energy to learn. So they do what they can, stick to the language they know, and hope for the best.

Unfortunately, hope is a lousy defense against the many issues that lie ahead:

annoyances

mistakes

frustrations

fears

dissatisfaction

boredom

incompatibility

temptations

regrets

troubles

Over time, couples discover that sticking to what they know works only for so long (if, indeed, it ever worked at all). No matter what they do, their best efforts never seem to be good enough. Their spouse never seems satisfied. The "in-loveness" that carried them to the altar dissipates, leaving two people who bear little resemblance to the starry-eyed lovebirds in their wedding photos.

Whether they verbalize it or not, husbands and wives who want to avoid divorce and stay together still face a choice. **Their first option is to lower their expectations and accept the new status quo.** They can choose to live with the diminishing returns of their relationship and stay together for a number of reasons.

They stick it out for the sake of the kids.

Staying married means less hassle and expense than splitting up.

They don't *hate* each other, exactly.

They want to avoid a major life change, which can be scary.

Their second option is to figure out what's wrong with the relationship and work to make it better. To refuse to settle for the status quo. To find new and creative ways of communicating love and affection for each other.

MAKING THE TOUGH CALL

The second option is the better one, but it's certainly not the easier one—especially if damage has already been done to the relationship. Every marriage has its ups and downs, of course. In some, however, the ups aren't quite as high as the couple imagined, and the downs are considerably lower and longer than they'd ever thought possible.

Over time, those lows—as well as the incidents and circumstances that caused them—can take a toll. **Past annoyances, disagreements, and mistakes become obstacles to intimacy.** The shrapnel damage from previous emotional warfare can leave spouses feeling too wounded to talk about their day, let alone try to communicate in an unfamiliar love language.

With their love tanks bone-dry or running on fumes, spouses allow resentment and anger to take hold. The question then becomes, how do they work their way through the emotional minefields they created together?

How do they begin to address years of heated words, regrettable choices, unresolved issues, and silent resentment?

They *choose* to.

Just as they chose to put those obstacles there in the first place—they *chose* to speak critical words; they *chose* to allow their emotions in the driver's seat; they *chose* to put other priorities ahead of their relationship—they can choose love.

The Right Words

Let's say you've made some choices you're not proud of, even though they may have seemed justified at the time. Let's say these choices are playing havoc with your relationship. What do you do? What do you say?

First, you acknowledge that you're not compelled to keep making these choices. You can opt for something different, something more beneficial for your marriage.

Second, you gather your courage and say to your wife, "I'm sorry. I know I've hurt you, but I would like to make the future different. I would like to love you in your language. I would like to meet your needs." I've seen countless marriages rescued from the brink of divorce when couples make the choice to love.

Love doesn't erase the past, but it can make the future different. When we choose to actively express love in the primary love languages of our wives, we create an emotional climate in which we can deal with our past conflicts and failures.

WHERE DID OUR LOVE GO?

Brent sat in my office, stone-faced and seemingly unfeeling. He hadn't come by his own initiative but at my request. A week earlier his wife, Becky, had been sitting in the same chair, weeping. Between her outbursts of tears, she managed to explain that Brent had told her that he no longer loved her and that he was leaving. She was devastated.

When she regained her composure, she said, "We've both worked so hard on our careers the last two or three years. I knew that we weren't spending as much time together as we used to, but I thought we were working for a common goal. I can't believe what he's saying. He's always been such a kind and caring person. He's such a good father to our children. How could he do this to us?"

I listened as she described their twelve years of marriage. It was a story I'd heard many times before. They had an exciting courtship, got married at the height of the in-love experience, had the typical adjustments in the early days of marriage, and pursued the American dream. In due time, they came down off the emotional high of the in-love experience but didn't learn to speak each other's love language sufficiently. She'd lived with a love tank only half full for the last several years, but she'd received enough expressions of love to make her think that everything was okay.

Brent's love tank, on the other hand, was empty. His outward appearance was in stark contrast to Becky's. She had been weeping, but he was stoic. I had the impression, however, that his tears had been shed weeks or perhaps months before—and that it had been an inward weeping. The story Brent told confirmed my hunch.

"I just don't love her anymore," he said. "I haven't loved her for a long time. I don't want to hurt her, but we're not close. Our relationship has become empty. I don't enjoy being with her anymore. I don't know what happened. I wish it were different, but I don't have any feelings for her."

Brent was thinking and feeling what countless other husbands have thought and felt through the years. It's the "I don't love her anymore" mindset that gives men the emotional freedom to seek love with someone else. The same is true for wives who use the excuse.

WHEN TWO PEOPLE FALL IN LOVE

I sympathized with Brent, because I've been there—feeling emotionally empty, wanting to do the right thing, not wanting to hurt anyone, but being pushed by emotional needs to seek love outside the marriage. Fortunately, I'd discovered in the early years of my marriage the difference between the in-love experience and the "emotional need" to feel loved. Most in our society have not yet learned that difference.

The in-love experience is practically instinctive. It's not premeditated; it simply happens in the normal context of male-female relationships. It can be fostered or quenched, but it doesn't arise by conscious choice. It's short-lived (usually two years or less) and seems to serve for humankind the same function the mating call does for the Canadian goose.

The in-love experience temporarily meets our emotional need for love. It gives us the feeling that someone cares, that someone admires us and appreciates us. Our emotions soar with the thought that another person sees us as *the one*, that she's willing to devote time and energies exclusively to our relationship. For a brief period, however long it lasts, our emotional need for love is met. Our tank is full. We can conquer the

> You can't plan to fall in love with someone. You can only go along for the ride.

world. Nothing is impossible. For many individuals, it's the first time they've ever lived with a full emotional tank, and it's euphoric.

In time, however, we come down from that natural high back to the real world. If our wife has learned to speak our primary love language, our need for love will continue to be satisfied. If, on the other hand, she doesn't speak our love language, our tank will slowly drain, and we'll no longer feel loved.

Meeting that need in one's spouse is definitely a choice. If I learn the emotional love language of my wife and speak it frequently, she will continue to feel loved. When she comes down from the obsession of the in-love experience, she will hardly even miss it because her emotional love tank will continue to be filled. However, if I haven't learned her primary love language or have chosen not to speak it, when she descends from the emotional high, she will have the natural yearnings of unmet emotional needs. After some years of living with an empty love tank, she will likely "fall in love" with someone else, and the cycle will begin again.

Meeting my wife's need for love is a choice I make each day. If I know her primary love language and choose to speak it, her deepest emotional needs will be met and she will feel secure in my love. If she does the same for me, my emotional needs will be met, and both of us will live with full love tanks. In a state of emotional contentment, both of us will give our creative energies to projects outside the marriage while we continue to keep our relationship exciting and growing.

RUNNING ON EMPTY

With all that in my mind, I looked back at the deadpan face of Brent and wondered if I could help him. I knew in my heart that he was probably already involved with another in-love experience. I wondered if it was in the beginning stages or at its height. Few men suffering from an empty emotional love tank leave their marriages until they have prospects of meeting that need somewhere else.

Brent was honest and revealed that he'd been in love with someone else for several months. He had hoped that the feelings would go away and that he could work things out with his wife. But the situation at home had gotten worse, and his love for the other woman had increased. He'd reached the point where he couldn't imagine living without his new lover.

I sympathized with Brent in his dilemma. He sincerely didn't want to hurt his wife or his children, but at the same time, he felt he deserved a life of happiness. I gave him the dismal statistics on second marriages. He was surprised to hear them but was certain that he would beat the odds. I told him about the research on the effects of divorce on children, but he was convinced that he would continue to be a good father to his children and that they would get over the trauma of the divorce. I talked to him about the issues in this book and explained the difference between the experience of falling in love and the deep emotional need to feel loved. I explained the five love languages and challenged him to give his marriage another chance.

All the while, I knew that my intellectual and reasoned approach to marriage compared to the emotional high that he was experiencing was like pitting a BB gun against an automatic weapon. He expressed appreciation for my concern and asked that I do everything possible to help Becky. But he declared that he saw no hope for the marriage.

One month later, I received a call from Brent. He asked to talk with me again. This time when he entered my office, he was noticeably disturbed. He was not the calm, cool man I'd seen before. His lover had begun to come down from the emotional high, and she was observing things in Brent that she didn't like. She was withdrawing from the relationship, and he was crushed. Tears came to his eyes as he told me how much she meant to him and how unbearable it was to experience her rejection.

I listened for an hour before Brent ever asked for my advice. I told him how sympathetic I was to his pain and indicated that what he was experiencing was the natural emotional grief from a loss, and that the grief would not go away overnight. I explained, however, that the experience was inevitable. I reminded him of the temporary nature of the in-love experience, that sooner or later, we always come down from the high to the real world. Some fall out of love before they get married; others, after they get married. He agreed that it was better now than later.

After a while, I suggested that perhaps the crisis was a good time for him and his wife to get some marriage counseling. I reminded him that true, long-lasting emotional love is a choice and that emotional love could be reborn in his marriage if he and his wife learned to love each other in the right love languages. He agreed to marriage counseling.

Fast-forward to nine months later. Brent and Becky left my office with a reborn marriage. When I saw Brent three years after that, he told me what a wonderful marriage he had and thanked me for helping him at a crucial time in his life. He told me that the grief over losing his other lover had been gone for more than two years. He smiled and said, "My love tank has never been so full, and Becky is the happiest woman you're ever going to meet."

Fortunately for Brent and his marriage, he had a brush with what I call the disequilibrium of the in-love experience. That is, **almost never do two people fall in love on the same day, and almost never**

do they fall out of love on the same day. You don't have to be a social scientist to recognize that truth. Just listen to an hour of country music. Brent's lover happened to have fallen out of love with him at an opportune time.

GETTING THE HANG OF IT

In the nine months that I counseled Brent and Becky, we worked through numerous conflicts that they'd never resolved before. But **the key to the rebirth of their marriage was discovering each other's primary love language and choosing to speak it frequently.**

"What if the love language of my spouse is something that doesn't come naturally for me?"

I'm often asked this question at my marriage seminars. My answer is, "So?"

My wife's love language is acts of service. One of the things I do for her regularly as an act of love is vacuum the floors. Do you think that vacuuming floors comes naturally for me? My mother used to make me vacuum. All through junior high and high school, I couldn't go play ball on Saturday until I finished vacuuming the entire house. In those days, I said to myself, "When I get out of here, there's one thing I'm never going to do again: I'm not going to vacuum my house. I'll get myself a wife to do that."

But I vacuum our house now, and I vacuum it regularly. And there's only one reason I vacuum our house. Love. You couldn't pay me enough to vacuum a house, but I do it for love. You see, when an action doesn't come naturally to you, it is a greater expression of love. My wife knows that when I vacuum the house, it's nothing but 100 percent pure, unadulterated love, and I get credit for the whole thing!

Someone might say, "But, Dr. Chapman, that's different. I know that my wife's love language is physical touch, but I'm not a toucher. I never saw my mother and father hug each other. They never hugged me. I'm just not wired that way. What am I going to do?"

Do you have two hands? Can you put them together? Now imagine that you have your wife in the middle and pull her toward you. I'll bet that if you hug your wife three thousand times, it will begin to feel more comfortable.

Ultimately, **our comfort isn't the issue**. We're talking about love, and love is something you do for someone else, not something you do for yourself. Most of us do many things each day that don't come "naturally" for us. For some of us, that list starts with getting out of bed in the morning. We go against our feelings and get out of bed. Why? Because we believe there's something worthwhile to do that day. And normally, before the day is over, we feel good about having gotten up. Our actions precede our emotions.

The same is true with love. When you discover the primary love language of your wife, you choose to speak it, whether or not it's natural or comfortable for you. You may not get warm, excited feelings while you're doing it, but that's okay. You're simply choosing to do it for her benefit. You want to meet your wife's emotional need, so you reach out to speak her love language. In so doing, her emotional love tank is filled, and chances are she'll reciprocate and speak your language. When she does, your emotions return, and your love tank begins to fill.

Love is a choice. And either partner can start the process today.

9

How Can You Work Through Anger Together?

---

nger, left unchecked, can disrupt the flow of love languages indefinitely. Before you can communicate genuine love and affection to your wife, you must

- address the flashpoint issues that cause conflict;
- come up with an effective plan for dealing with anger when it rears its head.

In this chapter, you'll find the tools, strategies, and encouragement to help you and your wife work through your feelings of anger—and strengthen your relationship in the process.

"I don't ever remember losing my temper until I got married." Dan may have been looking back at his bachelor years through rose-colored glasses, but he was certain of one thing: Sarah provoked his anger. "When she says certain things or gives me *that look,* I get furious."

Sarah's sarcastic questions bothered him. How's a guy supposed to respond when his wife asks, "Are you going to mow the lawn, or do I have to ask my father to come over and do it?"

And that wasn't even the worst of it, as far as Dan was concerned. Sometimes Sarah would tilt her head a certain way and stare at him. "That look is worse than a thousand condemning words," Dan confided in me. "What I see in her eyes is, 'I'm sorry I married you.'"

Dan was angry because Sarah struck at his self-esteem—a particularly vulnerable spot. **Most of us want to be liked, accepted, appreciated, and respected. So when we're criticized, we tend to respond defensively.** Sarah may argue that she's criticizing Dan's *behavior*, not his person. But since our behavior is an extension of who we are, it's difficult for most of us, including Dan, to make the distinction. Something deep within Dan said, "It's not right for my wife to put me down."

The tone of Sarah's voice made it clear that she too was angry. She'd concluded that Dan wasn't doing his fair share around the house. From her perspective, the grass grew taller while he went to the gym. He watched TV while she carried out the garbage.

Not exactly her idea of a loving husband.

Dan and Sarah's situation is hardly unique. All married couples deal with anger issues. And that's okay. **There's nothing wrong with experiencing anger.** The problem is, many couples have never learned how to process it productively. Instead, they explode in tirades that do nothing but make the situation worse. Or they suffer in silence and withdraw from each other.

How many of us can look back on our childhood and remember outings that were spoiled not by weather but by our parents' anger toward each other? How many birthdays have been ruined by the bickering of parents who haven't learned to resolve their anger? How many holidays have become days of misery because of anger run rampant?

Unfortunately most married adults have never learned how to handle anger properly. As a result, marriage becomes a battlefield, with each spouse accusing the other of firing the first shot. Until the couple learns to properly handle their anger, they'll never have a satisfying marriage. Their efforts to learn each other's love language will never pay dividends. I say *never* because **love and uncontrolled anger cannot coexist.** Love seeks the well-being of the spouse, while uncontrolled anger seeks to hurt and destroy.

SIX KEYS TO ANGER MANAGEMENT

The good news is that couples can learn to handle anger responsibly. In fact, they *must* learn this if they are to survive and thrive. It's not an easy process, but the results are certainly worth the effort.

Let's break it down into six steps.

1. Acknowledge the reality of anger.

When two people become one and attempt to build a life together, anger is inevitable. Some anger will be *definitive*, stimulated by wrong action on the part of a spouse. Some anger will be *distorted*, sparked by a misunderstanding of what happened. The average married couple will experience a fair share of both types of anger. That's just the by-product of living life with a fallible human being.

There's nothing inherently morally wrong about anger. It's simply evidence of our concern for fairness and justice. **When we sense something**

> One of the most loving gifts you can give your wife is the freedom to feel anger toward you.

is unfair or unjust, anger is our natural reaction. There's no need to condemn ourselves or our wife for experiencing anger. Likewise, there's no need to deny being angry. There's no shame in it.

When we give each other the right to feel anger, we're actually giving each other the right to be human. This is the starting place in learning to process anger positively.

2. Agree to acknowledge your anger to each other.

When you are angry, give your wife the benefit of *knowing* what you're feeling (or if your wife is angry, allow her to tell you how she feels). Don't play "Guess My Mood." Such guessing games are a waste of time. Even worse, they rarely produce an accurate answer.

If you're angry toward your wife, it's because she's done or said something that you believe is inappropriate—or because she's failed to do or say something that you expected. As far as you're concerned, she's done you wrong. She's treated you unkindly. Unfairly.

Unlovingly.

In that moment, the event that triggered your anger has become a barrier between the two of you. Your wife deserves to know that. She can't work on a problem she's unaware of.

Each spouse deserves to know when the other is angry and what they're angry about. A husband and wife who commit to giving each other this information have taken a major step toward resolving anger productively.

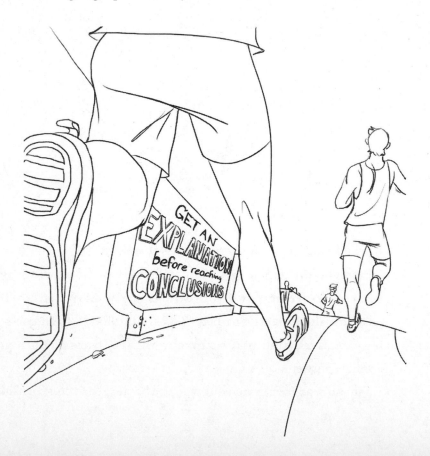

3. Agree that verbal or physical explosions that attack the other person are not appropriate responses to anger.

The unhealthy venting of anger is *always* destructive and should not be accepted as appropriate behavior. That doesn't mean that once you and your wife make the agreement neither of you will ever lose your cool again. What it means is that you're committed to acknowledging that the response was wrong. **Explosive expressions of anger *always* make things worse.** And the emotional debris from those explosions must be cleared before you can deal constructively with the incident that triggered the anger.

One practical way to break the habit is to agree that whenever either of you begins to explode, the other will walk out of the room. If the exploder follows, the spouse will walk out of the house . . . into the yard . . . around the block, if necessary. And the walking away won't stop until the exploding does.

If you both agree to that strategy, you'll know that when one of you leaves the room—or house—it's time to stop and reflect on what's happening. Ideally, when the mobile spouse returns from the walk, the angry spouse will have calmed down—and will have the humility and presence of mind to say, "I'm sorry. My exploding at you was wrong. I guess I was so hurt and angry that I lost control. Please forgive me." If the two of you can reconcile after that momentary lapse of control, you can get to the issue that originally caused the anger.

4. Agree to seek an explanation before passing judgment.

If you're angry with your wife, your first impression is that her behavior is wrong. Just make sure you treat it as a first impression—and not a confirmed fact—until you hear her side of the

story. It's all too easy to misinterpret someone's words or actions.

Let's say your wife didn't come home with the gallon of milk you asked her to buy—even after she wrote a note to herself as a reminder. The knee-jerk reaction to her oversight would be to get angry at her apparent irresponsibility. But what if the store was out of milk? What if she drove a coworker home from the office and didn't go past a store? What if she knew you didn't need milk for dinner and planned to pick it up on her way to take your daughter to gymnastics? All plausible explanations. And **if you're committed to seeking an explanation, you'll withhold your judgment of irresponsibility until you get her perspective.**

Rob overheard his wife on the phone say that "he was late" and that she "couldn't stand being late." He felt angry because he'd made every effort to be there on time and was only two minutes late. When he asked his wife for an explanation, he found that she was actually talking about a friend's baby who arrived two weeks late. Crisis averted.

The next time you're convinced that your wife has done something to make you angry, ask yourself if you've ever been wrong before.

If actions and words are open to misunderstanding, motives are even more difficult to guess. Since motives are internal, we can never know our wife's reason for doing something unless she tells us. Unfortunately, we often attribute motives to our wife that are totally off base.

Jonathan was acting wisely when he said, "I may be misreading this, and that's why I'm asking for an explanation. It looks to me like you charged $300 at Macy's. I thought we agreed that neither of us would spend over $100 without consulting the other until we get our debts under control." He was stunned by Bethany's response.

"Oh, honey, I can explain. Our department at work went in together to buy Betsy a retirement gift. They asked me to pick it up during my lunch hour since I was meeting Ginger at the mall. So I put the whole thing on Visa. But they each gave me $20. It's in my purse. I think I have $300." Jonathan's anger subsided as he counted the $300.

5. Agree to seek a resolution.

In the case of Jonathan and Bethany, Jonathan's anger was resolved once he received Bethany's explanation. Obviously not all anger resolution is that easy. Not all incidents turn out to be misunderstandings. Let's assume that Bethany *had* actually broken their commitment and made a $300 purchase after agreeing that neither of them would purchase anything over $100 without discussing it with the other. Let's assume her explanation was, "But, honey, it was on sale. I saved $200, and we need it. I didn't think you would object."

> A quick, heartfelt exchange of "I love yous" after a bout with anger will strengthen your relationship and protect it from fallout.

"Well, I do object," Jonathan replies. "It would be nice to have it, but we don't really need it. We've gotten along pretty well without it. And we can't afford to add $300 to our debt. We made an agreement, and you broke it. I think that's wrong."

That kind of direct, loving confrontation opens the door to all kinds of constructive conversation and problem solving.

6. Agree to affirm your love for each other.

After the anger is resolved, say to each other with all sincerity, "I love you." What you're really saying is, "I'm not going to allow this incident to separate us." As a couple, you've heard each other out, resolved the issue, learned from the experience, and agreed to move on together.

In situations where a true wrong has been committed—where one spouse has been unkind, unloving, or unjust—an admission of the wrongdoing and a change of behavior are in order. So is forgiveness, from the spouse who was wronged. At that point, the anger ignited by the incident can go dormant again, having served its purpose of holding both spouses accountable for their behavior.

If the anger turns out to be distorted—the result of a misunderstanding—a different approach must be taken. After setting the record straight, the spouse who jumped to conclusions should be big enough to own up to their mistake. The couple can then talk about the circumstances that led to the misunderstanding and brainstorm some ideas for avoiding the situation in the future.

Few things are more important to a successful marriage than learning to resolve anger in a responsible manner. I believe a genuine commitment to these six principles will set you and your wife on a path toward responsible anger management.

As if You Needed More Reasons . . .

Evidence from the world of academia that anger can be hazardous to your health:

An Ohio State study found that a thirty-minute marital spat can add a day—or more—to the time it takes a physical wound to heal.

A Harvard study reported that older men inclined to explosive anger are at three times greater risk of a heart attack than their calmer peers.

IS THIS A GOOD TIME TO TALK?

Let me close this chapter with one final suggestion. On an index card, write the following words:

I'm feeling angry right now, but don't worry. I'm not going to attack you. But I do need your help. Is this a good time to talk?

Put the card on your bathroom mirror or in some other accessible place. The next time you feel anger toward your wife, read the card aloud to her as calmly as you can. If it turns out not to be a good time to talk, set a time for later.

In this brief statement, you've acknowledged that you're experiencing anger, you've affirmed your commitment not to explode, and you've expressed your desire for an explanation and resolution through conversation.

When you sit down to discuss the issue, begin by saying, "I know that I could be misunderstanding this. That's why I wanted to talk to you. Let me tell you what I'm feeling and why. Then if you can straighten the situation out, I'd appreciate it, because I need help in resolving it." An opening like that creates a nonthreatening atmosphere in which the two of you can discuss the situation.

Anger will make occasional visits to every household. But we need not dread its arrival. **Anger can be a friend.** It can play a valuable role in your relationship. It can bring you and your wife together in ways other emotions can't. Every time the two of you work through a bout of anger, you strengthen your relationship a little more.

SIX STEPS FOR DEFUSING AN ANGRY CONFRONTATION

The next time an anger-causing situation arises, try working through these steps with your wife. For maximum effectiveness, you should have these steps in place in your relationship *before* the situation arises.

1. **Acknowledge the reality of anger.** Whether your anger is definitive (legitimate) or distorted, refuse to condemn yourself for experiencing it. Recognize and admit to your anger. Remember, anger itself is not wrong.

2. **Agree to acknowledge your anger to each other.** Express clearly your feeling of anger when it arises. Don't make your wife

guess based on your behavior. Both you and your wife deserve to know when the other is angry and what the cause of the anger is.

3. **Agree that verbal or physical explosions against the other person are not appropriate responses to anger.** Either kind of explosion will only make things worse.

4. **Agree to seek an explanation before passing judgment.** Remember, your first impression may be faulty. It's easy to misinterpret your wife's words and actions. Before you jump to conclusions, get her perspective. She may supply valuable missing information that changes your understanding of the situation.

5. **Agree to seek a resolution.** With more information from your wife and a fuller perspective, you're ready to find a solution that's satisfactory for both of you. Resolving the angry feelings may require an admittance of the wrongdoing and a change of behavior from your wife, if the wrongdoing is valid and definitive. If it turns out your anger is distorted or unwarranted, you will be the one who needs to admit your wrongdoing and change your behavior.

6. **Agree to affirm your love for each other.** After the anger is resolved, verbally—and sincerely—declare your love for each other.

The Art of Apologizing

Do you have a go-to tool on your workbench? One that feels just right in your hand? One you reach for first when you've got a job to do?

How about a go-to move on the basketball court? Something you save for crunch time, when you really need to shake a defender or score a bucket? Perhaps a crossover dribble at the top of the key or a step-back three-pointer?

Or maybe you have a go-to strategy in chess—an opening gambit that often catches your opponents off guard.

The right go-to move can snatch victory from the jaws of defeat. The right go-to strategy can mean the difference between success and failure.

In the past few chapters, we've talked about the obstacles that can derail your plans to become fluent in your wife's primary love language—and cool her desire to become fluent in yours.

You can't prevent the temptations and frustrations that will threaten your intimacy. You can't take back harsh words that have already been spoken. You can't undo mistakes that have already been made.

But with one action—one go-to move—you can take a giant stride toward strengthening your relationship, restoring intimacy, and creating incentives for learning each other's love language.

If your objective is to make things right with your wife, your go-to move is the apology.

Done well, an apology can bring closure to tensions, conflicts, and hurt feelings that have been sore spots for months, even years. It can **change the way your wife thinks of you**—the way she looks at you. It can **break down barriers** faster than any other words or actions can.

The question is, what does it take to do an apology well?

What most people look for in an apology is sincerity. They want the apology to be genuine. The problem is, people have different ideas of what constitutes sincerity. What one person considers to be sincere is not what another person considers to be sincere.

In my years of counseling and leading seminars for married couples, I've discovered that just as there are five languages of love, **there are also five languages of apology**. For most people, one or two of these languages convey sincerity more effectively than the others do.

In order for an apology to be accepted by your wife, you need to speak the language or languages that best convey your sincerity to her. With that in mind, let's take a look at the five languages of apology.

Like This Chapter? You'll Love the Book.

If you'd like to know more about the five languages of apology, pick up the book *When Sorry Isn't Enough* by Gary Chapman and Jennifer Thomas.

In it, you'll find thought-provoking discussions of the

importance of apologies in your marriage, in your family, and in your workplace, as well as practical tips on how to forgive someone who's wronged you, how to forgive yourself, and how to teach your children to apologize.

APOLOGY LANGUAGE #1: EXPRESSING REGRET

Expressing Regret is the emotional aspect of an apology. Regret focuses on what you did (or failed to do) and how it affected the other person—in this case, your wife. **To express regret to your wife is to acknowledge your own sense of guilt, shame, and pain about your behavior that has hurt her so deeply.**

If your wife has been wounded deeply, she will want you to feel some of her pain. That's not necessarily vindictiveness at work. She simply wants assurance that *you* know how she's feeling. Words of genuine regret provide that assurance.

A simple "I'm sorry" can go a long way toward restoring goodwill after an offense. The absence of the words "I'm sorry" will stand out to some people like a Packers jersey at a Bears home game. Quite often, the husband offering the apology won't realize he's left out those two magic words. But you can bet his wife will realize it. That's why **the best strategy is to lead with them—to begin every apology with a sincere "I'm sorry."**

Of course, sincerity is measured by more than just words. Your body language must also convey your regret.

If you didn't say "I'm sorry," you didn't apologize.

Jim teared up when he apologized to his wife.

Robert looked his wife in the eyes and held her gaze when he expressed his regret.

"I know that I hurt you. I feel like a jerk for causing you pain. I'm truly sorry for what I did."

"I'm sorry I offended your parents, but it's not like you show them a lot of respect."

"I'm sorry I used that language with you, but I never claimed to be a choirboy."

"The last thing I want to do is disappoint you. I should have been more thoughtful. I'm sorry for making you feel that way."

Sean shook his head in annoyance, rolled his eyes, and let out a heavy sigh when he said "I'm sorry" to his wife.

Guess whose wife didn't believe his apology was sincere?

In addition to being sincere, **an apology should be specific**. "I'm sorry for _____." The more details you give, the better you communicate to your wife that you understand the depth of what made her upset. The more you understand, the less chance there is of repeating the offense in the future.

By being specific, you also give your wife the opportunity to clarify her feelings. If you say, "I'm sorry for making us late to the school program," your wife may surprise you by saying, "That's not what upset me. On Saturday, when we were getting ready to go to the movie, you kept hurrying all of us, saying you hated to be late to movies. I'm upset that you don't seem to have that same urgency when it comes to our kids' band performances."

Words of sincere regret also need to stand alone. **Under no circumstance should they be followed by the word *but*** ("I'm sorry I said you remind me of my mother . . . *but* sometimes you push me too far"). Any time you verbally shift the blame to your wife, you move from an apology to an attack. Attacks never lead to forgiveness and reconciliation. Likewise, any time you follow an apology with an excuse ("I'm sorry I scheduled a round of golf on our anniversary, but you're better at remembering that stuff than I am"), you cancel out the apology.

If you want your wife to sense your sincerity, then you must learn to speak the apology language of regret. You must learn to focus on how your behavior is related to her pain. Your recognition of her pain will likely inspire her to forgive you.

APOLOGY LANGUAGE #2: ACCEPTING RESPONSIBILITY

Why is it so difficult for some of us to say, "I was wrong"? Often our reluctance to admit to wrongdoing is tied to our sense of self-worth. To admit that we are wrong is perceived as weakness. We may reason, *Only losers confess. Intelligent people try to show that their actions were justified.*

So we rationalize. We gloss over *what* we did and focus on the why.

That rationalization often takes the form of blaming others. We may admit that what we said or did wasn't necessarily good or right. But we're quick to point out that our behavior was provoked by someone else's irresponsible actions. We shift responsibility to someone else because we find it difficult to say, "I was wrong."

That's a big problem because **for many people, hearing the words "I was wrong" is what communicates to them that an apology is**

"Mistakes were made.
Let's just leave it at that."

"I'm sorry you're upset, but it's not like I
haven't done it before. That's just who I am."

"The way I spoke to you was wrong. I was trying
to justify myself, and what I said was unkind
and unloving. I hope you will forgive me."

"I could try to excuse myself, but there
is no excuse. Pure and simple, what I
did was selfish and wrong."

sincere. If your wife falls into that category, she will not accept your apology as being genuine if it doesn't contain words that accept responsibility for your wrong behavior. Understanding this reality can make all the difference in the world when you sincerely wish to apologize for your behavior.

"My husband will not admit that he ever does anything wrong. He just sweeps it under the rug and doesn't want to talk about it anymore. If I bring it up again, he will say, 'I don't know what I did. Why can't you just forget it?' If he could admit that it was wrong, I would be willing to forgive him. But when he acts like he did nothing wrong, it's really hard to overlook it. I just wish I could hear him say one time, 'I was wrong.'"

—Jenna

"My husband, Michael, is the most honest man I've ever met. I don't mean he's perfect. I mean he's always willing to admit his failures. I guess that's why I love him so much, because he has always been willing to say, 'I made a mistake. I was wrong. Will you forgive me?' I like a person who is willing to accept responsibility for his mistakes."

—Lizzy

"I never heard my father apologize to my mother or to me. I felt that my father was hypocritical. In the community he was recognized as a successful man, but in my mind he was a hypocrite. I guess that's why I have always been quick to apologize, willing to admit my failures. I want my relationships to be genuine, and I know that can't happen if I'm not willing to admit that I was wrong."

—Mike

For these individuals and many others, hearing the apology language of Accepting Responsibility for one's wrong behavior is the most important part of an apology. It is what convinces these individuals that the apology is sincere. As one person put it, "'I'm sorry' is not enough. I want to know that he understands that what he did was wrong."

If your wife is one who would echo that sentiment, you will be well served to become fluent in the apology language of Accepting Responsibility.

APOLOGY LANGUAGE #3: MAKING RESTITUTION

The idea of "making things right" after doing something wrong is embedded in our human psyche. Both our judicial system and our interpersonal relationships are deeply influenced by this fundamental

"I don't feel right just saying 'I'm sorry.' I want
to make up for what I've done. What would you
consider appropriate?"

"I know that I've wasted your time. May I give
you some of my time to balance things out?"

"Why can't you let it go? I bought you flowers!
Isn't that enough?"

"If saying 'Sorry' isn't good enough for you, I
don't know what to tell you."

idea. In recent years, the American judicial system has given more emphasis to the concept of reparative damages, the idea that criminals should repay their victims for the damages caused by the criminals' behaviors. Rather than simply spending time in prison, the criminal is required to make up for his or her wrong to the person who was wronged.

The idea of reparative damages is based on the innate human sense that **when a wrong has been committed, it should be "paid for."** That concept is also the basis of the third apology language: Making Restitution.

In the private sphere of marriage, our desire for restitution is almost always based on our need for love. **After being hurt deeply, we need the reassurance that the spouse who hurt us still loves us.**

Harsh words or hurtful actions call love into question.

"How could she do that to me?" is the question that lingers in our minds. The words "I'm sorry; I was wrong" may not be enough. We want to know the answer to the question, "Do you still love me?"

For some people, Making Restitution is a primary apology language. As far as they're concerned, "I'm sorry" must always be accompanied by something along the lines of "What can I do to show you that I still love you?" Without this effort at restitution, they will question the sincerity of the apology. They will continue to feel unloved no matter how many times you say, "I was wrong."

As for what they expect?

"I expect some sense of contrition, but also a sincere effort to amend the damage caused by the rift."

"I expect him to try to repair what's gone wrong."

"I expect her to be truly sorry from the heart and be willing to make things right."

All these people viewed the effort to make restitution as the strongest evidence of the sincerity of the apology. The question is, how do we make restitution in the most effective way? Since the heart of restitution is reassuring your wife that you genuinely love her, **it's essential to express restitution in her primary love language**.

For some people, words of affirmation—being told how wonderful or incredible they are in conjunction with the apology—is all the restitution they need.

For some people, acts of service—vacuuming the floor, washing dishes, doing laundry—prove the sincerity of an apology.

For some people, gift giving—something that shows they were being thought of—says "I'm sorry" like nothing else.

For some people, quality time—giving your undivided attention while you apologize—is restitution enough.

For some people, nothing speaks more deeply of love than physical touch. For them, an apology without physical contact is insincere.

Whatever your wife's love language is, keep this in mind: **A genuine apology will be accompanied by a desire to right the wrongs that were committed, to make amends for the damage done, and to assure your wife that you genuinely care about her.**

APOLOGY LANGUAGE #4: GENUINE REPENTANCE

"We have the same old arguments about the same old things." The woman who shared that analysis with me had been married for nearly thirty years. "I think that's true of most couples. What upsets me most is not what he does; it's that he does it over and over again. He apologizes. He promises not to do it again. Then he does it again, whether it's leaving the bathroom light on or being crabby and unpleasant. I don't want any more apologies. I want him to stop doing the things that bother me—for good."

This woman wanted her husband to repent.

The word *repentance* means "to turn around" or "to change one's mind." In the context of an apology in your marriage, it means that you realize your present behavior is destructive. You regret the pain you're causing your wife, and you choose to change your behavior.

Repentance is more than saying, "I'm sorry; I was wrong. How can I make this up to you?" To repent is to say, "I'll try not to do this again." For some people, repentance is what convinces them that an apology is sincere.

Without Genuine Repentance, the other languages of apology may fall on deaf ears. What people who have been hurt want to know is, "Do you intend to change, or will this happen again next week?"

"I'm sorry. I know I said that before, but this time I'm serious. Trust me."

"I know that my behavior was very painful to you. I don't ever want to do that again. I'm open to any ideas you might have on how I can change my behavior."

"I let you down by making the same mistake again. What would it take for you to begin to rebuild your trust in me?"

"I am sorry. But if the things I do keep offending you, maybe you're the one who needs to change. Did you ever think about that?"

The language of Genuine Repentance is what causes people to describe an ideal apology like this:

"Show that you're willing to change, and do things differently next time."

"I expect him to find ways to keep it from happening again."

"I expect a change of behavior so that the insult doesn't recur."

"I want him to have a plan for improvement, a plan to succeed and not fail again."

"I expect him not to go into a rage a few minutes later or do the same thing again."

These and countless other statements reveal that for many people, repentance is at the heart of a true apology.

How then do we speak the language of repentance? **It begins with an expression of intent to change.** All true repentance begins in the heart. We recognize that what we've done is wrong, that our actions have hurt the one we love. We don't want to continue this behavior, so we decide that we will change. Then we verbalize this decision to the person we've offended—in this case, our wife.

This decision to change indicates that we are no longer making excuses. We are not minimizing our behavior but are accepting full responsibility for our actions.

When you share your intention to change with your wife, you are communicating to her what's going on inside you. You're giving her a glimpse into your heart. And often that is enough to convince her that you mean what you say.

APOLOGY LANGUAGE #5: REQUESTING FORGIVENESS

Requesting Forgiveness is important for three reasons. First, **it indicates that you want to see your relationship restored**. Ron and Nancy have been married for fifteen years, and Ron acknowledges that his primary apology language is Requesting Forgiveness. "When she asks me to forgive her, I know she doesn't want to sweep it under the rug. She wants our relationship to be authentic. Whatever else she says in her apology, I know that when she gets to the place where she asks me to forgive her that she is totally sincere. That's why she makes it easy for me to forgive her. I know that she values our relationship more than anything. That makes me feel really good."

When an offense occurs, it immediately creates a barrier between spouses. Until that barrier is removed, the relationship can't go forward. An apology is an attempt to remove the barrier. If you discover your wife's primary language is Requesting Forgiveness, then this is

"Last time I looked, only God has the power
to forgive. I said I was sorry. If that's not good
enough, I don't know what to tell you."

"I'm sorry for the way I spoke to you.
I know it was loud and intense. You didn't
deserve that. It was very wrong of me, and
I want to ask you to forgive me."

"I wish you would quit playing the victim.
So you got hurt. Boo hoo. Life goes on.
Get over it!"

"I know that what I did hurt you very deeply.
You have every right never to speak to me again,
but I am truly sorry for what I did. And I hope that
you can find it in your heart to forgive me."

the surest way of removing the barrier. To her, this is what indicates that you genuinely want to see the relationship restored.

A second reason that Requesting Forgiveness is important is that **it shows that you realize you have done something wrong**—that you have offended your wife, intentionally or unintentionally. What you said or did may not have been morally wrong. You have done or said it as a joke. But it offended your wife. She now holds it against you. The offense has created a rift between the two of you. In that sense, it is wrong, and Requesting Forgiveness is in order—especially if it's your wife's primary apology language. Asking for forgiveness is an admission of guilt. It shows that you know you deserve some degree of condemnation or punishment.

Third, **Requesting Forgiveness shows that you are willing to put the future of your relationship in the hands of your wife**—the offended person. You have admitted your wrong. You have expressed your regret. You may even have offered to make amends. But now you're saying, "Will you forgive me?" You know that you can't answer that question for your wife. It's a choice she must make. To forgive or not to forgive, that is the question. And the future of your relationship rests on her decision. This takes the control out of your hands, something that's very difficult for many people to accept.

Verbally asking for forgiveness after you've expressed an apology using some of the other apology languages often is the key that opens the door to the possibility of forgiveness and reconciliation. It may be the one element of your apology that your wife is waiting to hear.

"Will you please forgive me?" is the ingredient that convinces her that you are indeed sincere in your apology. Without the request for forgiveness, your statements such as "I'm sorry," "I was wrong," "I'll make it up to you," and "I'll never do it again" may sound like glib remarks to her. If Requesting Forgiveness is your wife's primary apology language, then you must learn to speak it if you want her to know that your apology is genuine.

THE LAST WORD

The art of apologizing is not easy. It doesn't come naturally to most people, but it can be learned by all. And it's worth the effort. Apologizing opens up a whole new world of emotional and spiritual health. Having apologized, we are able to look ourselves in the mirror—and look our wives in the eyes.

Remember, those who sincerely apologize are most likely to be truly forgiven.

For a free online study guide, please visit
www.5lovelanguages.com

Frequently Asked Questions

1. What if I can't discover my primary love language?

"I've taken the Love Language Profile and my scores come out almost even except for gift giving. I know that's not my primary love language. What should I do?"

In the book, I discuss three approaches to discovering your love language.

- First, observe how you most often express love to others. If you're regularly doing acts of service for others, this may be your love language. If you're consistently verbally affirming people, then words of affirmation is likely your love language.

- Second, consider what you complain about most often. When you say to your wife, "I don't think you'd ever touch me if I didn't initiate it," you're revealing that physical touch is your primary love language. When your wife goes on a shopping trip in the city and you say, "You didn't bring me anything?" you're indicating that gift giving is your love language. The statement "We don't ever spend time together" indicates the love language of quality time. Your complaints reveal your inner desires. (If you have difficulty remembering what you complain about most often, ask your wife. She'll know.)

- Third, think of the requests you make of your wife most often. If you're saying, "Will you give me a back rub?" you are asking for physical touch. "Do you think we could get a weekend away this month?" is a request for quality time. "Would it be possible for you to clean out your closet this afternoon?" expresses your desire for acts of service.

One husband told me that he discovered his love language by simply following the process of elimination. He knew that gift giving was not his language, so that left only four. He asked himself, "If I had to give up one of the four, which one would I give up first?" His answer was quality time. "Of the three remaining, if I had to give up another, which one would I give up?" He concluded that apart from sexual intercourse, he could give up physical touch. He could get along without the pats and hugs and holding hands. That left acts of service and words of affirmation. While he appreciated the things his wife did for him, he knew that her affirming words were really what gave him life. He could live for a whole day on one positive comment from her. That's how much they meant to him. It was no stretch to conclude that words of affirmation was his primary love language and acts of service was his secondary love language.

2. What if I can't discover my wife's love language?

"My wife hasn't read the book, but we have discussed the love languages. She says she doesn't know what her love language is."

My first suggestion is to give your wife a copy of *The 5 Love Languages: The Secret to Love That Lasts*. If she reads it, she'll likely be eager to share her love language with you. However, if she doesn't have the time or interest to read the book, I would suggest you answer variations of the three questions discussed in question #1.

- How does your wife most often express love to others?
- What does she complain about most often
- What does she request most often?

Though your wife's complaints may sometimes irritate you, they're actually giving you valuable information. If your wife says, "We don't ever spend any time together," you may be tempted to say, "What do you mean? We went out to dinner Thursday night." Such a defensive statement will end the conversation. If, on the other hand, you respond, "What would you like for us to do?" you'll likely get a helpful answer. Your wife's complaints are the most powerful indicators of her primary love language.

Another approach is to do a five-week experiment. The first week, you focus on one of the five love languages and try to speak it every day. Observe your wife's response. On Saturday and Sunday, you relax. The second week—Monday through Friday—you focus on another of the love languages. Continue with a different language each of the five weeks. On the week you speak your wife's primary love language, you'll likely see a difference in her countenance and the way she responds to you. It will be obvious that this is her primary love language.

3. Does your primary love language change as you get older?

I think our primary love language tends to stay with us for a lifetime. It's like many other personality traits that develop early and remain consistent. For example, a highly organized person was likely organized as a child. A person who is laid-back and relaxed likely had those traits as a child. This is true of numerous personality traits.

However, there are certain situations in life that make the other love languages extremely attractive. For example, your primary love language may be words of affirmation, but if you're working two jobs, then acts of service by your wife may become extremely attractive to you. If she gives you only words of affirmation and doesn't offer to help you with household responsibilities, you may begin to think, "I'm tired of hearing you say 'I love you' when you never lift a hand to help me." For the time you're working two jobs, it may seem as though acts of service has become your primary love language. However, if your wife's words of affirmation stopped, you'd quickly realize that it was still your primary love language.

If you experience the death of a parent or a close friend, an extended hug by your wife may be the most meaningful thing for you at the moment—even if physical touch isn't your primary love language. There's something about being held in the midst of our grief that communicates that we're loved. So while physical touch isn't your primary love language, it can be very meaningful on certain occasions.

4. Does the five love language concept work with children?

Most definitely. Inside every child there's an emotional love tank. If children feel loved by their parents, they will grow up normally. But if their love tanks are empty, they will grow up with many internal struggles. During the teenage years they'll likely go looking for love, often in the wrong places. For that reason, it's extremely important that parents learn how to love children effectively. Some time ago, I teamed up with psychiatrist Ross Campbell to write *The 5 Love Languages of Children*. The book is written for parents and is designed to help them discover their child's primary love language. It also discusses how that love language interfaces with the child's anger, the child's learning, and the child's discipline.

One of the points we make in the book is that children need to learn how to receive and give love in all five languages. This produces an emotionally healthy adult. Thus, parents are encouraged to give heavy doses of the child's primary love language, then sprinkle in the other four regularly. When children receive love in all five languages, they will eventually learn how to give love in all five languages.

5. Do children's love languages change when they get to be teenagers?

A parent said, "I've read *The 5 Love Languages of Children*, and it really helped us in raising our children. However, now our son has become a teenager. We're doing the same things we've always done, but it doesn't seem to be working. I'm wondering if his love language has changed."

I don't believe a child's love language changes at age thirteen. However, you must learn new ways to speak the child's primary love language. Whatever you've been doing in the past, the teenager considers it childish and wants nothing to do with it.

If the teen's love language is physical touch and you've been hugging him and kissing him on the cheek, he may well push you away and say, "Leave me alone." It doesn't mean that he doesn't need physical touch; it means that he considers those particular touches to be childish. You must now speak physical touch in more adult dialects, such as an elbow to the side, a fist to the shoulder, or a pat on the back. Or you might wrestle your teen to the floor. These touches will communicate your love to a teenager. The worst thing you can do to a teenager whose love language is physical touch is to withdraw when the teen says, "Don't touch me."

For more on relating to teens, see *The 5 Love Languages of Teenagers.*

6. What if the primary love language of your wife is difficult for you?

"I didn't grow up in a touching family, and now I've discovered that my wife's love language is physical touch. It's really difficult for me to initiate it."

The good news is that all five love languages can be learned. It's true that most of us grew up speaking only one or two of these love languages. These will come natural for us and will be relatively easy to speak. The others must be learned. As in all learning situations, small steps make for big gains.

If physical touch is your wife's language and you're not by nature a "toucher," begin with small things such as putting your hand on her shoulder as you pour a cup of coffee or give her a "love pat" on the shoulder as you walk by. These small touches will begin to break down the barrier. Each time you touch, the next touch will be easier. You can become proficient in speaking the language of physical touch.

The same is true with the other languages. If you're not a words of affirmation person and you discover that your wife's language is words of affirmation, make a list of statements that you hear from other people or that you read or hear in the media. Stand in front of a mirror and read the list until you become comfortable hearing yourself say those words. Then choose one of the statements to say to your wife. Each time you affirm her, it will become easier. Not only will your wife feel good about your changed behavior but you'll also feel good about yourself, because you'll know that you're effectively expressing love to her.

7. Are some of the love languages found more among women and others found more among men?

I've never done the research to discover if certain love languages are gender-slanted. Anecdotal evidence suggests that more men have physical touch and words of affirmation as their love language and more women have quality time and gift giving. But I don't know if that's statistically accurate.

I prefer to deal with the love languages as being gender-neutral. I do know that any one of the five love languages can be the primary love language of a man or the primary love language of a woman. The important thing in marriage is that you discover the primary and secondary love languages of your spouse and speak them regularly. If you do that, you will create a healthy emotional climate for marital growth.

8. **How did you discover the five love languages?**

    For years, I helped couples in the counseling office discover what their spouse desired in order to feel loved. Over time, I began to see a pattern in their responses. I discovered that what makes one person feel loved does not necessarily make another person feel loved. I read over the notes I'd made and asked myself this question: "When someone sat in my office and said, 'I feel like my spouse doesn't love me,' what did that person want?" The answers fell into five categories. I later called them the five love languages.

    I started sharing these languages in workshops and study groups. When I did, I saw the lights come on for couples who suddenly realized why they had been missing each other emotionally. When they discovered and spoke each other's primary love language, it radically changed the emotional climate of their marriage.

    I decided to write a book in which I would share the concept, hoping to influence other couples whom I would never have an opportunity to meet in person. Now that the book has sold over nine million copies in English and has been translated into fifty languages around the world, my efforts have been more than rewarded.

9. **Do the love languages work in other cultures?**

    Since my academic background is anthropology, this was my question when a Spanish publisher first requested permission to translate and publish the book in Spanish. I initially said, "I don't know if this concept works in Spanish. I discovered it in an Anglo setting."

The publisher said, "We've read the book, and it works in Spanish." Then came the French edition, the German, the Dutch, and many more. In almost every culture, the book has become a bestseller of the publisher. This leads me to believe that these five fundamental ways of expressing love are universal.

However, the *dialects* in which these languages are spoken will differ from culture to culture. For example, the kinds of touches that are appropriate in one culture may not be appropriate in another. The acts of service that are spoken in one culture may not be spoken in another. But when these cultural adaptations are made, the concept of the five love languages will have a profound impact on the couples in that culture.

10. Why do you think *The 5 Love Languages* has been so successful?

I believe that our deepest emotional need is the need to feel loved. If we're married, the person we would most like to love us is our spouse. If we feel loved by our spouse, the whole world is bright and life is wonderful. On the other hand, if we feel rejected or ignored, the world begins to look dark.

Most couples get married when they still have the euphoric feelings of being "in love." When the euphoric feelings evaporate sometime after the wedding and the couple's differences begin to emerge, they often find themselves in conflict. With no positive plan for resolving conflicts, they resort to speaking harshly to each other. Harsh words create feelings of hurt, disappointment, and anger. Not only do the husband and wife feel unloved but they also begin to resent each other.

When couples read *The 5 Love Languages*, they discover why

they lost the romantic feelings of courtship and how emotional love can be rekindled in their relationship. Once they begin speaking each other's primary love language, they are surprised to see how quickly their emotions turn positive. With a full love tank, they can process their conflicts in a much more positive manner and find solutions that are workable.

The rebirth of emotional love creates a positive emotional climate between them, and they learn to work together as a team—encouraging, supporting, and helping each other reach meaningful goals.

Once this happens, they want to share the message of the five love languages with all their friends. I believe the success of *The 5 Love Languages* can be attributed to the couples who have read it, learned to speak each other's language, and recommended it to their friends.

11. What if I speak my wife's love language and she doesn't respond?

"My wife wouldn't read the book, so I decided to speak her love language and see what would happen. Nothing happened. She didn't even acknowledge that I was doing anything differently. How long am I supposed to continue speaking her love language when there's no response?"

I know that it can become discouraging when you feel that you're investing in your marriage and receiving nothing in return. There are two possibilities as to why your wife is not responding. First, and most likely, you're speaking the wrong love language.

Many husbands assume that their wife's love language is acts of service. So they start tackling projects around the house. They check off items on the household to-do list at a furious pace. They are sincerely trying to speak their wife's love language. When she doesn't even acknowledge the efforts, her husband may become discouraged.

In reality, her primary love language may be words of affirmation. Because her husband feels no love coming from her, he may be verbally critical of her. His critical words are like daggers to her heart, so she withdraws from him. She suffers in silence while he becomes frustrated that his efforts for improving the marriage are unsuccessful. The problem is not his sincerity; the problem is that he's actually speaking the wrong love language.

On the other hand, assuming you are speaking your wife's primary love language, there is another reason why she may not be responding positively. If she is already involved in another romantic relationship, either emotionally or sexually, she will often reason that your efforts have come too late. She may even perceive that your efforts are temporary and insincere and that you're simply trying to manipulate her to stay in the marriage. Even if your wife isn't involved with someone else, if your relationship has been hostile for a long time, she may still perceive your efforts as being manipulative.

In this situation, the temptation is to give up, to stop speaking her love language because it's not making any difference. The worst thing you can do is to yield to this temptation. If you give up, it will confirm her conclusion that your efforts were designed to manipulate her.

The best approach you can take is to continue to speak her love language on a regular basis no matter how she treats you. Set yourself a goal of six months, nine months, or a year. Your attitude should be, *No matter what her response is, I'm going to love her in her love language over the long haul. If she walks away from me, she will walk away from someone who is loving her unconditionally.* This attitude will keep you on a positive path even when you feel discouraged.

There is nothing more powerful that you can do than to love your wife even when she's not responding positively. Whatever the ultimate response of your wife, you will have the satisfaction of knowing that you've done everything you could do to restore your marriage. If your wife eventually chooses to reciprocate your love, you will have demonstrated for yourself the power of unconditional love. And you will reap the benefits of the rebirth of mutual love.

12. Can love be reborn after sexual infidelity?

Nothing devastates marital intimacy more than sexual unfaithfulness. Sexual intercourse is a bonding experience. It unites two people in the deepest possible manner. Almost all cultures have a public wedding ceremony and a private consummation of the marriage in sexual intercourse. Sex is designed to be the unique expression of our commitment to each other for a lifetime. When this commitment is broken, it is devastating to the marriage.

However, this does not mean that the marriage is destined for divorce. If the offending party is willing to break off the extramarital involvement and do the hard work of rebuilding the marriage, there can be genuine restoration.

In my own counseling experience, I've seen scores of couples who have experienced healing after sexual infidelity. It involves not only breaking off the extramarital affair but also discovering what led to the affair in the first place.

Success in restoration is a two-pronged approach. First, the offending party must be willing to explore their own personality, beliefs, and lifestyle that led them to the affair. There must be a willingness to change attitudes and behavior patterns. Second, the couple must be willing to take an honest look at the dynamics of their marriage and be open to replacing destructive patterns with positive patterns of integrity and sincerity. Both of these solutions will normally require the help of a professional counselor.

Research indicates that the couples who are most likely to survive sexual infidelity are those couples who receive both individual counseling and marriage counseling. Understanding the five love languages and choosing to speak each other's language can help create an emotional climate in which the hard work of restoring the marriage can be successful.

13. What do you do when your wife refuses to speak your love language even though she knows it?

"We both read *The 5 Love Languages*, took the profile, and discussed our primary love languages with each other. That was two months ago. My wife knows that my love language is words of affirmation. Yet in two months, I have yet to hear her say anything positive. Her love language is acts of service. I've started doing several things she's asked me to do around the house. I think she appreciates what I'm doing, but she never tells me."

Let me begin by saying that we cannot make our spouse speak our love language. Love is a choice. We can request love, but we cannot demand it. Having said that, let me suggest some reasons why your wife may not be speaking your love language.

She may have grown up in a home where she received few

positive words. Her parents were perhaps very critical of her. Thus, she did not have a positive role model when it comes to speaking words of affirmation. Such words may be very difficult for her to verbalize. It will require effort on her part and patience on your part as she learns to speak a language that's foreign to her.

A second reason that she may not be speaking your love language is that she fears that if she gives you words of affirmation for the few changes you've made, you'll become complacent and not go on to make the major changes she's hoping for. It is the mistaken idea that if I reward mediocrity, I will curtail the person's aspirations to be better. That is a commonly held myth that keeps some parents from verbally affirming children. Of course, it's untrue. If a person's primary love language is words of affirmation, those words challenge the person to greater levels of accomplishment.

My suggestion is that you initiate the love tank game discussed in chapter 7. You ask her, "On a scale of zero to ten, how full is your love tank?" If she answers anything less than ten, you ask, "What could I do to help fill it?" Whatever she says, do it to the best of your ability. If you do this once a week for a month, chances are she will start asking you how full your love tank is. And you can begin making requests of her. This is a fun way of teaching her how to speak your love language.

14. Can emotional love return after it's been gone for thirty years?

"We're not enemies. We don't fight. We simply live in the same house like roommates."

Let me answer this question with a true story. A couple came to me at one of my seminars. The husband said, "We've come to thank you for bringing new life to our marriage. We've been married for thirty years, but the last twenty years have been extremely empty. If you want to know how bad our marriage has been, we haven't taken a vacation together in twenty years. We simply live in the same house, try to be civil, and that's about it.

"A year ago, I shared my struggle with a friend. He went into his house, came back with your book *The 5 Love Languages* and said to me, 'Read this. It will help you.' The last thing I wanted to do was read another book, but I did. I went home that night and read the whole book. I finished about 3:00 a.m., and with every chapter, I realized that we had failed to speak each other's love language through the years.

"I gave the book to my wife and asked if she would read it and tell me what she thought of it. Two weeks later, she said, 'I read the book.' 'What did you think about it?' I asked. 'I think if we had read that book thirty years ago, our marriage would have been very different.' I said to her, 'That's the same thought I had. Do you think it would make any difference if we tried now?' She responded, 'We don't have anything to lose.'

"We discussed our primary love languages and agreed that we would try to speak each other's language at least once a week to see what would happen. If anyone had told me that in two months I would have love feelings for her again, I would never have believed it. But I did."

His wife spoke up and said, "If anyone had told me that I would ever have love feelings for him again, I would have said, 'No way. Too much has happened.'" She then said, "This year we took our first vacation together in twenty years and had a wonderful time. We drove four hundred miles to come to your seminar and enjoyed being with each other. I'm just sad that we wasted so many years of simply living in the same house when we could have had a love relationship. Thank you for your book."

"Thank you for sharing your story," I said. "I find it greatly encouraging. I hope you make the next twenty years so exciting that the last twenty will be a dim memory."

"That's what we intend to do," they both said together.

Can emotional love be reborn in a marriage after thirty years? Yes, if the two of you are willing to try speaking each other's love language.

15. I'm single. How does the love language concept apply to me?

Through the years, many single adults have said to me, "I know you wrote your original book for married couples. However, I read it and it helped me in all my relationships. Why don't you write a book on the five love languages for singles?" And so I did. It's titled *The 5 Love Languages for Singles*. In the book, I try to help single adults apply the love language concept in all their relationships. I begin by helping them understand why they felt love or did not feel love growing up as a child.

One young man who is incarcerated said, "Thanks for sharing the five love languages. For the first time in my life, I finally understand that my mother loves me. I realize that my love language is physical touch, but my mother never hugged me. In fact, the first hug I ever remember getting from my mother was the day I left for prison. But I realize that she spoke acts of service very strongly. She worked hard to keep us in food and clothes and to provide a place to live. I know now that she loved me; she simply wasn't speaking my language. But now I understand she really did love me."

I also help singles apply the love language concept in their sibling relationships, work relationships, and dating relationships. I have been extremely encouraged by the response of single adults. I hope that if you're single, you'll discover what others have discovered. Expressing love in a person's primary love language enhances all relationships.

16. How do I speak my spouse's love language if he or she is away from me for a time (e.g., deployment, work, school)?

I am frequently asked how to apply the five love languages in long-distance relationships. Physical touch and quality time are particularly challenging in these instances. The simple answer is this: you must be creative and committed to staying connected despite the distance.

If your love language is physical touch, then here are a few creative ideas for speaking one another's love language. First, having photographs of yourself as a couple may remind you of enjoyable times together. Having physical items that belong to one another may also remind you of each other. Perhaps a shirt or the cologne or perfume of your significant other may remind you of that person and of enjoyable times together. You also should email, text, write, etc., about how you enjoy being with one another. You might even try keeping a calendar on which you physically mark off the days until you're able to be together again. This is not a comprehensive list of ideas, but all of these are physical activities and items that will at least in part help satisfy your physical love language.

As for quality time, the time you spend staying in contact, working to encourage one another, sending each other notes and gifts, etc., is quality time. Of course, it's not the preferred form of quality time, but it is quality time nonetheless. You must learn to view it and appreciate it as such.

More specific ways you can express the language of quality time are to talk often about how you desire to stay close and keep your love alive. Read or reread *The 5 Love Languages* (or *The 5 Love Languages Military Edition*) together while you're apart, or listen to Dr. Chapman's podcasts, and discuss these together as a way of nurturing your relationship. This, too, requires commitment, but if you truly love one another, then you'll find the energy and time to stay connected.

Use your situation as an opportunity to practice the other languages as well. Notes and gifts need to be viewed as more than "just" notes and gifts. They need to be viewed as physical effort and words of affirmation meant to express love.

In closing, yes, distance is difficult on a relationship, but it does not have to be the end of the relationship. Obviously, the more time you can spend together, the better. And, you should strive for this. However, if you are a committed couple and are willing to be creative in how you speak one another's love language, then your relationship can survive and even thrive during your time apart.

The 5 Love Languages® *Profile for Couples—for Him*

The 5 Love Languages® Profile will give you and your spouse or significant other a thorough analysis of your emotional communication preference. It will single out your primary love language, what it means, and how you can use it to connect with your loved one with intimacy and fulfillment. Two profiles are included so that each of you can complete the assessment.

You will now see 30 paired statements. Please select the statement that best defines what is most meaningful to you in your relationship as a couple. Both statements may or may not sound like they fit your situation, but please choose the statement that captures the essence of what is most meaningful to you the majority of the time. Allow 10 to 15 minutes to complete the profile. Take it when you are relaxed, and try not to rush through it. Then tally your results and learn how to interpret your profile on page 184.

It's more meaningful to me when . . .

1
| I receive a loving note/text/email for no special reason from my loved one. | A |
| she and I hug. | (E) |

2
| I can spend alone time with her—just the two of us. | (B) |
| she does something practical to help me out. | D |

3
| she gives me a little gift as a token of our love for each other. | C |
| I get to spend uninterrupted leisure time with her. | (B) |

4
| she unexpectedly does something for me like filling my car or doing the laundry. | D |
| she and I touch. | (E) |

5
| she puts her arm around me when we're in public. | (E) |
| she surprises me with a gift. | C |

6
| I'm around her, even if we're not really doing anything. | (B) |
| we hold hands. | E |

7
| my loved one gives me a gift. | C |
| I hear "I love you" from her. | (A) |

8
| I sit close to her. | E |
| I am complimented by her for no apparent reason. | (A) |

It's more meaningful to me when . . .

9

I get the chance to just "hang out" with her. (B)

I unexpectedly get small gifts from her. C

10

I hear her tell me, "I'm proud of you." (A)

she helps me with a task. D

11

I get to do things with her. B

I hear supportive words from her. (A)

12

she does things for me instead of just talking about doing nice things. D

I feel connected to her through a hug. (E)

13

I hear praise from her. (A)

she gives me something that shows she was really thinking about me. C

14

I'm able to just be around her. (B)

I get a back rub or massage from her. E

15

she reacts positively to something I've accomplished. (A)

she does something for me that I know she doesn't particularly enjoy. D

16

she and I kiss frequently. (E)

I sense she is showing interest in the things I care about. B

It's more meaningful to me when . . .

17
my loved one works on special projects with me that I have to complete. Ⓓ

she gives me an exciting gift. C

18
she compliments me on my appearance. Ⓐ

she takes the time to listen to me and really understand my feelings. B

19
we share nonsexual touch in public. Ⓔ

she offers to run errands for me. D

20
she does a bit more than her normal share of the responsibilities we share (around the house, work-related, etc). Ⓓ

I get a gift that I know she put thought into choosing. C

21
she doesn't check her phone while we're talking. Ⓑ

she goes out of her way to do something that relieves pressure on me. D

22
I can look forward to a holiday because of a gift I anticipate receiving. C

I hear the words, "I appreciate you" from her. Ⓐ

23
she brings me a little gift after she has been traveling without me. C

she takes care of something I'm responsible to do but I feel too stressed to do at the time. Ⓓ

It's more meaningful to me when . . .

24

she doesn't interrupt me while I'm talking.   B

gift giving is an important part of our relationship.   Ⓒ

25

she helps me out when she knows I'm already tired.   D

I get to go somewhere while spending time with her.   Ⓑ

26

she and I are physically intimate.   Ⓔ

she gives me a little gift that she picked up in the course of her normal day.   C

27

she says something encouraging to me.   Ⓐ

I get to spend time in a shared activity or hobby with her.   B

28

she surprises me with a small token of her appreciation.   C

she and I touch a lot during the normal course of the day.   Ⓔ

29

she helps me out—especially if I know she's already busy.   D

I hear her specifically tell me, "I appreciate you."   Ⓐ

30

she and I embrace after we've been apart for a while.   E

I hear her say how much I mean to her.   Ⓐ

The 5 Love Languages® Profile for Couples—for Her

Here is the second profile. As previously mentioned, it will give you a thorough analysis of your emotional communication preference. It will single out your primary love language, what it means, and how you can use it to connect with your loved one with intimacy and fulfillment. Two profiles are included so that each of you can complete the assessment.

You will now see 30 paired statements. Please select the statement that best defines what is most meaningful to you in your relationship as a couple. Both statements may or may not sound like they fit your situation, but please choose the statement that captures the essence of what is most meaningful to you the majority of the time. Allow 10 to 15 minutes to complete the profile. Take it when you are relaxed, and try not to rush through it. Then tally your results and learn how to interpret your profile on page 184.

A - 6   B - 7   C - 1

It's more meaningful to me when . . .

1

I receive a loving note/text/email for no special reason from my loved one. (A)

he and I hug. E

2

I can spend alone time with him—just the two of us. B

he does something practical to help me out. (D)

3

he gives me a little gift as a token of our love for each other. C

I get to spend uninterrupted leisure time with him. (B)

4

he unexpectedly does something for me like filling my car or doing the laundry. (D)

he and I touch. E

5

he puts his arm around me when we're in public. E

he surprises me with a gift. (C)

6

I'm around him, even if we're not really doing anything. (B)

we hold hands. E

7

my loved one gives me a gift. C

I hear "I love you" from him. (A)

8

I sit close to him. (E)

I am complimented by him for no apparent reason. A

D-12   E·4

It's more meaningful to me when . . .

9
I get the chance to just "hang out" with him. (B)
I unexpectedly get small gifts from him. C

10
I hear him tell me, "I'm proud of you." A
he helps me with a task. (D)

11
I get to do things with him. B
I hear supportive words from him. (A)

12
he does things for me instead of just talking about doing nice things. (D)
I feel connected to him through a hug. E

13
I hear praise from him. (A)
he gives me something that shows he was really thinking about me. C

14
I'm able to just be around him. B
I get a back rub or massage from him. (E)

15
he reacts positively to something I've accomplished. A
he does something for me that I know he doesn't particularly enjoy. (D)

16
he and I kiss frequently. E
I sense he is showing interest in the things I care about. (B)

It's more meaningful to me when . . .

17
my loved one works on special projects with me that I have to complete. — D

he gives me an exciting gift. — C

18
he compliments me on my appearance. — A

he takes the time to listen to me and really understand my feelings. — B

19
we share nonsexual touch in public. — E

he offers to run errands for me. — D

20
he does a bit more than his normal share of the responsibilities we share (around the house, work-related, etc). — D

I get a gift that I know he put thought into choosing. — C

21
he doesn't check his phone while we're talking. — B

he goes out of his way to do something that relieves pressure on me. — D

22
I can look forward to a holiday because of a gift I anticipate receiving. — C

I hear the words, "I appreciate you" from him. — A

23
he brings me a little gift after he has been traveling without me. — C

he takes care of something I'm responsible to do but I feel too stressed to do at the time. — D

It's more meaningful to me when . . .

24

he doesn't interrupt me while I'm talking. (B)

gift giving is an important part of our relationship. C

25

he helps me out when he knows I'm already tired. (D)

I get to go somewhere while spending time with him. B

26

he and I are physically intimate. (E)

he gives me a little gift that he picked up in the course of his normal day. C

27

he says something encouraging to me. A

I get to spend time in a shared activity or hobby with him. (B)

28

he surprises me with a small token of his appreciation. C

he and I touch a lot during the normal course of the day. (E)

29

he helps me out—especially if I know he's already busy. (D)

I hear him specifically tell me, "I appreciate you." A

30

he and I embrace after we've been apart for a while. E

I hear him say how much I mean to him. (A)

Look back through the letters you circled and record the number of responses in the spaces below.

A:__11__ B:__7__ C:__1__ D:__3__ E:__8__

A = Words of Affirmation   **B** = Quality Time   **C** = Gift Giving
D = Acts of Service   **E** = Physical Touch

INTERPRETING YOUR PROFILE SCORE

The highest score indicates your primary love language (the highest score is 12). It's not uncommon to have two high scores, although one language does have a slight edge for most people. That just means two languages are important to you.

The lower scores indicate those languages you seldom use to communicate love and which probably don't affect you very much on an emotional level.

IMPORTANT TO REMEMBER

You may have scored more highly on certain love languages than others, but do not dismiss those other languages as insignificant. Your partner may express love in those ways, and it will be helpful to you to understand this about him.

In the same way, it will benefit your spouse or significant other to know *your* primary love language in order to best express affection for you in ways that you interpret as love. Every time you or he speaks each other's language, you score emotional points with each other. Of course, this isn't a game with a scorecard! The payoff of speaking each other's love language is a greater sense of connection. This translates into better communication, increased understanding, and, ultimately, improved romance.

If your spouse or significant other has not already done so, encourage him or her to take *The 5 Love Languages®* Profile in this book, online (5lovelanguages. com/profile or on *The 5 Love Languages®* app (iOS or Android). Discuss your respective love languages, and use this insight to improve your relationship!

Acknowledgments

I am deeply indebted to the men who have opened their hearts to me through the years. Some of them have sat in my office, and others I have met while leading marriage seminars across the country. They are sincere men who want to have a successful marriage but admit that they don't know how to make that happen. It has been my pleasure to be a part of their journey toward a growing marriage.

For this revised edition I deeply appreciate the help of Randy Southern and Chris Hudson. Also, as always, I express my heartfelt gratitude to the Northfield Publishing team: John Hinkley, Betsey Newenhuyse, and Zack Williamson.

STRENGTHEN YOUR RELATIONSHIPS

ONLINE

DISCOVER YOUR LOVE LANGUAGE AND MORE AT

www.5lovelanguages.com

OTHER WAYS TO CONNECT:

 /5lovelanguages

 /drgarychapman

 /drgarychapman

 /user/drgarychapman

BRUTAL BOSSES.
POISONOUS PEOPLE.
SOUL-CRUSHING CULTURES.

THIS BOOK WILL GIVE YOU THE CONFIDENCE
TO RISE ABOVE THEM ALL.

A SMALL FABLE

WITH GREAT WISDOM

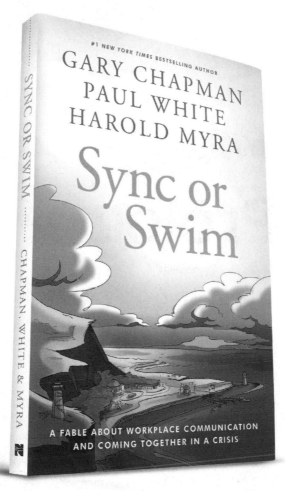

Sync or Swim

A Fable About Workplace Communication
and Coming Together in a Crisis

appreciationatwork.com/syncorswim